ALL NATURE SINGS: *A Spiritual Journey of Place*

ALL NATURE SINGS

Published in the United States by Credo House Publishers,
a division of Credo Communications, LLC, Grand Rapids, Michigan.
www.credocommunications.net

ISBN-13: 978-1-935391-40-1

Photo Credits:
Cover, pages 124 and 159 by Jessica Miller
All other photos by Fritz M. Rottman

*To the dreamer who invited me
to become his prairie-partner.*

*And to others who encounter God in creation's astonishing splendor
in places like Flat Iron Lake Preserve.*

Yellow Prairie Coneflowers

PREFACE

You hold in your hands a travel journal—not to exotic parts of the globe or to scenes of known beauty—just to my backyard. Granted, the yard is a seventy-acre tract divided between woods, a lake and wide-open fields. Every day I walk down the quarter-mile driveway to get the mail and the newspaper. Along the way I gather a collection of sightings and musings in this place and among the living things that inhabit this land—the place I now too call home.

If you were to view the landscape from the top down, a Google™ Earth vantage point rather from my horizontal look, you'd see Hart Street, an east/west main road with a slightly curved driveway leading from it, crossing the field ending in a lasso-like loop in front of our house.

The size and shape of the lake would come up as a dark oval with a tail. The tree lines would show as diffused gray—one huge band of woods on the west, a narrow strip along the lakeshore to the east and another around a large swale north of the drive. A lighter shade indicates the vegetable garden and paths leading from the house outward. If you walked with me from the road to the house, you would not see the lake until we went around or through the house, which is on the highest spot of land next to the water.

Flat Iron Lake and the land surrounding it has become my habitat. I dwell in this place not of my own making. I live in time chosen for me. I am a single soul trying to be faithful to my calling. Like many a journey, the direction it takes is not known at the onset. Our driveway always leads to the mailbox, but my thoughts will carry me to unfamiliar places. So I invite you to come with me on this pilgrimage of sorts. Discover the mysteries, and yes the magic, along this uncharted journey of place.

November

"Lord, you have assigned me my portion and my cup;
You have made my lot secure.
The boundary lines have fallen for me in pleasant places;
Surely I have a delightful inheritance."

Psalm 16:5-6 (NIV)

Milkweed Pod

ALL NATURE SINGS: A SPIRITUAL JOURNEY OF PLACE

Novomber's starkness surprises me each day as I walk down my long and winding driveway to pick up the mail from our rural mailbox. The fields and the woods beyond are only a pale reminder of their former glory. Where once color bombarded me, only the brown-grays of dead plants show themselves. The colored leaves quickly brown and crunch underfoot, and the tall trees sway naked and black in the breeze. The sky, too, has lost its brilliant blues, as clouds darken to a diffused gray. All living things prepare for winter's chill. What an odd month to launch a nature journey.

Hard frost came last week, announcing that the time of growing, at least in Michigan, has passed. At each previous frost warning, my husband and I tried to extend the season by covering plants with old sheets and tarps. Finally, I made my rounds of the fragile plants, picking a few peppers, a handful of green beans and boxes of hard, green, never-to-vine-ripen tomatoes. The raspberries that gave their all from August through October now want nothing more than to die back and store up their vitality for next year. We dug the carrots and then buried them below the frost line for use during the winter. Sweet potatoes, a new crop this year, yielded abundantly—fat, twisted potatoes, with no market or aesthetic value, still cook sweet and fleshy. But cold does not kill everything, and the broccoli, kohlrabi, tender lettuce and spinach will continue to bear, slowly. Until the snow mats everything down, we love to pick, cook and savor each morsel from our own garden.

So why does someone like me decide to begin a nature journal just when plants die back and most living creatures hibernate or go south? Or to write of blooms long gone? Simply because every day of the year I see or remember something remarkable as I walk the driveway or the trail through the woods or along the mowed path around the perimeter of our land. During the growing season I gather mental notes to hang in my storehouse, waiting for inspection. Winter's short days are a perfect time to dredge my reserves for sightings of glory.

There is a time for everything, and a season for every activity under heaven: a time to be born and a time to die, a time to plant and a time to uproot.

Ecclesiastes 3:1-2

When I told a friend about my vow to walk the quarter-mile drive every day to get the paper, he asked, "Even in winter?" "Oh, especially in winter," I answered, remembering that when we moved to this place I had vowed never to take the car to get the prize at the end of the drive. "Oh, yea," he mocked, "You never stop at the box when you're driving back from town?" Well—"never say never," my mom used to say. But this I know: I must leave my cozy world at least once every day, even in God-awful weather. Winter displays a beauty all its own. I want to walk in it and let its magic startle me.

First thing each morning I take a short outdoor jaunt; Jake, our black Lab, has to go out, giving me a perfect excuse. Here in the country he needs no leash and could easily do without me. His homing instincts are strong, especially when breakfast waits inside. But I feel the need to gauge the day's weather fare in person. My husband, who prefers to get his weather news from the storm team on TV, always asks, "What's it like out there?" So I try to describe the way it felt as I walked along the drive in the half-light. He considers my assessment before planning any outdoor chores for the day.

My trips outside in all kinds of weather punctuate my days. From the capital letter of the sun finally popping above the lake's horizon to the period that marks its disappearance over the woods in the late afternoon, I fill up the day's middle at my desk—separated from even the senses of outdoors. In my study, the light seeps in over my shoulder as I work, but I am shielded from the calling crows or the running deer—those gorgeous elements in nature that always distract me. For a while, I see only the blank page or the waiting computer screen. I count on my sensory memory to bring forward each image so as to color the words. I rely on the breath of God to give life to my earth-bound, knowledge-limited words.

I believe along with essayist Patricia Hampl that we don't merely have experiences but are entrusted with them—that we need to do something with them. Showers of blessing—as I have inherited in this place—must not be allowed to seep into the ground and disappear. On days when I doubt—not only my gifts but also my will to use them—I take an extra walk down the driveway or across the field—searching for something I can neither handle nor hold. Often I hear the Spirit's wordless voice urging me to be a good steward of this land, these gardens and my words: "Help others see what you see and be where you've been."

I cannot store last season's sunshine in a box or the wild-flower blooms in everlasting vases. In winter, I cannot witness a maple's color, a catbird's song or garden mint. So, I pray that memory of their sight, sound and taste will linger. Winter is my best time for writing. Garden work is over, spontaneous picnics wait for warm days, and folks don't stop to see the fields of wildflowers. But it is my growing season. In the lull, I am full.

GARDEN WATCH | *I married a dreamer*

Not that I knew that when I was first attracted to him—in fact, he hid it nicely. Nor would I have known as a young coed that a dreamer was just what I needed. In the late '50s, as we studied together in the Calvin College library, I realized that Fritz was hard-working, smart and funny, but that he also had his worries. Over time they came out: Will I make the grade in grad school? Will I get tenure as a professor? Can we afford those house payments? But the dreamer in him also showed itself. Part of his success as a biochemist came because he could imagine some of the unknowns of how living systems worked. He was coloring outside the lines before anyone had coined that phrase. Many of our adventures as a family came because he could always imagine a future beyond our present state or place.

Fritz demonstrated a deep yearning for land and for growing things, even during his early days amid the industrial paper mills that polluted the air in Muskegon, Michigan. His family lived in a very modest place, hemmed in by houses on either side. But their narrow lot stretched "out back" past his mother's flower garden, the garage, his dad's work shed and the fenced-in vegetable garden to a ridge leading to a steep hill. As a kid, he would scuttle down the incline and explore the wilds beyond. Mature oaks and a small stream bounded his side of the "gully," from which he could see celery plants growing in the rich bottomland beyond.

So I shouldn't have been surprised—after nine years of marriage and three children, a string of rental apartments, and his first real job—when he began dreaming of a piece of land where there would be room for all of us to grow. One day he called me excitedly: "You've got to see this, Carol!" Through a colleague at Michigan State University, he had gotten a tip about some tracts of land for sale bordering the Red Cedar River—the same meandering river that runs through the campus. He fell in love with the barren piece of land close to a tree-lined stream and helped me imagine a house and garden and maybe even fruit trees and beehives. I didn't protest because I had no competing dream. We bought the field. We raised our three kids on Sylvan Glen Road, bounded on one side by the river and on the other by railroad tracks. We cultivated most of our land into gardens and grass, but beyond the end of our dirt road virgin woods and fields invited us to explore.

Sixteen years later, with two of our children in college, we decided to leave that place to take up work in the city of Cleveland. We couldn't have known how much we were leaving behind; we were forced by a poor housing market to buy a house in a populated suburb, with traffic racing by day and night on a one-way boulevard. The house sat on what I called a civilized acre with room for a garden once several large trees had been removed to allow for full sun. The beehives came along but didn't do well in the city, perhaps because of too few blooms and too much lawn fertilizer. At first Fritz was too busy in his new job and I in graduate school to lament our lost land. But unbeknownst to me, the dreamer was already imagining other land and water. He made the best of city living, for eighteen years cultivating remarkable gardens in a park-like backyard. His dream languished until he took early retirement.

All things being equal, we would have retired in Colorado—my home state, which both of us loved. But our children were having children, and they all lived in Michigan within a twenty-mile radius, a situation most grandparents covet. So the hunt was on—for a tract of land near water in rural Michigan. I must admit that my dreams, even within his parameters, have always been pint-sized. But I knew the day would come when he'd call excitedly from somewhere in Michigan saying, "You've got to see this, Carol."

NATURE WATCH | *Where are the deer?*

One of the first questions visitors ask is "What do you do about the deer?" Most folks who like wild places realize that deer also live there and can make a mess of most gardens. Karen, a long time friend with her own experience living in rural Michigan, gave us a book which lays out a detailed strategy for deer proofing your yard and garden: a seven-foot fence of two electrified wire strands on top and a foot-high band of chicken wire on the bottom. The mesh wire is two-foot high but one foot is buried below ground, to keep out the burrowing critters. Once set up, you "invite" deer to have a look by putting peanut butter on the shiny foil attached to the fence wire. They come, get a little shock and never come back again.

Long ago we disarmed the fence. But the deer do not return. The warning shock has been imprinted and passed from generation to generation!

Places of the Heart

"Don't worry. I'll be back. You know how I love the mountains!" were my last words to my mother as I left Denver in 1956 to attend college in Michigan. Had it not been for my dad's deep and oft-spoken desire for all five of his children to attend his alma mater, I might have stayed put beside the Rocky Mountains forever. All I knew of Michigan came from several trips to stay with my aunties, Mom's five sisters, during muggy summers. Some of my aunts were farmers' wives, so I got my first feel of collecting eggs from a hen house, bringing lunch to sweaty harvesters and watching my cousins play ball on hardpacked fields. I saw Lake Michigan from a distance but never even got my big toe wet.

One of those summers while my sister Mary and I were away in Michigan, my parents discovered an old Victorian house in the ghost town of Marble, Colorado, about 200 miles from Denver. The house, abandoned for years, with no amenities and in disrepair, was located in the heart of the Crystal River Valley. The dramatic Treasury Mountain range towered all around. My dad, an OB doc, loved the place because of its distance from Denver and the babies he would have to deliver, even while on vacation, if he were anywhere nearby. When we sisters returned, the decision had already been made: Marble would be our home every August and for holidays and trips in between. Mom remembers my reluctance about such primitive living; I remember only the beginning of a love affair with the place.

The mountains, especially those up close and accessible, tugged at my heart, no matter where I was. And they continued to do so long after I had made a commitment that pretty much sealed my Michigan home base. Fritz and I married after college and moved to Ann Arbor for graduate school. Years later we had one chance to move to Colorado with an early job offer but decided that Fritz's aging parents needed us nearby. But we made a pact, which has held for all these years, to travel to Colorado every year. While our children were growing up, we went for as much of August as we could manage, but now we go whenever the quaking aspen or bubbling Crystal River or the rough mountain roads call us.

I tell this story only so that you'll understand that retiring in Michigan represented the end of that "I'll be back" fantasy. Mine was not so much a dream as a longing for some mysterious unknown that home represented. That old house in Marble had become for me a symbol of simple living and peace. Several times in writing workshops I've been asked to return home in memory—to walk around in it, to name the people and the shops and the streets, and when a specific memory grabs to write it down. Memory has never brought me back to other houses, only to that little clapboard house in the mountains where I came of age in the middle '50s. It was there beside a rushing stream called Carbonate that I sat to write for the first time. I knew the meaning of "Rocky Mountain High" before John Denver had begun crooning those words. My senses were being filled as never before by each splash and the way the sun highlighted driftwood and rocks. My spirit levitated.

Would my senses be filled at this new place beside Flat Iron Lake in Michigan? The irony of flat was not lost on me. Could this land and its smooth-topped lake ever become a place of the heart for me?

November, 2004
Creation Groans

We know that the whole creation has been groaning as in the pains of childbirth right up to the present time. (Romans 8:22)
As I walk down the long driveway to pick up the mail, I can almost hear the earth groaning. Fall rains and the first dusting of snow have flattened the fields that so recently bloomed with wildflowers and grasses. Next year's seeds are in hibernation, waiting for the right time to reassert themselves. On the perimeter of the rolling land, the trees, too, have dropped their color in order to store energy for the time when sun and rain and temperatures are again favorable to new growth. I feel a certain sadness from the loss of visible life but am reassured that the potential for growth remains—even under the dried leaves and the matted stalks of the season just past.

Only a few months ago, this quarter-mile walk to the main road offered more pleasure than an English garden. But here no walls surrounded, nothing was manicured, and the arrangement of color remained haphazard. The weather conditions had seemed perfect, with the flowers arriving much earlier than usual and in greater abundance. As each new species

Downny Woodpecker

began to bloom, it needed longer and longer stalks to get enough light for its buds, as though to out-dazzle the others. Walking near or through the field on paths my husband had mowed, I often felt as though a door had opened into a secret garden.

Now I thrive on the hope of next year's greens and blooms, even as the landscape browns, then grays and disappears under white. Looking over the field today, I remember the summer we moved temporarily to Ann Arbor from Cleveland so my husband could get radiation treatments for prostate cancer. One night we took a slow walk alongside the Huron River and came across the sign Prairie Restoration.

"If I survive, that's what I want to do!" he insisted in his weakened state. Fritz quietly began to research just what it would take to reclaim the prairie on land somewhere in Michigan.

After treatment ended and his prognosis brightened, his brother called one day to say that he'd found some acreage for sale in the area where we wanted to relocate after retirement. Fritz couldn't wait to drive the five hours to see it. At first I was not impressed—just a field with corn stalks taller than I. But my husband could see this land's treasure long before I caught the vision, and he proceeded to sell all that he had to buy the field (see Matthew 13:44). Before long he was supervising the building of a house on a point of land overlooking Flat Iron Lake, as well as beginning the arduous task of prairie restoration. With the help of the Division of

BOOKS

Nature journal tracks changing seasons

BY ANN BYLE
THE GRAND RAPIDS PRESS

Carol Rottman thought she would be in Colorado for her retirement years, living, perhaps, in the small town of Marble where her parents had owned a vacation home. Instead, Rottman and her husband Fritz settled on considerable acreage on an east-west road between Rockford and Greenville, close to their children and grandchildren.

They moved to their property on Flat Iron Lake in 1999 and, by 2000, had cleared 17 acres and seeded those barren fields with native Michigan prairie grasses and wildflowers. Rottman began walking the quarter mile to the mailbox, making note of plants or animals or trees she hadn't noticed before.

"Every day I walk down the driveway and across our land, of journaling— and everything's new because and finally coming to terms I'm a city girl. I see something and try to figure it out," with the fact said Rottman. "I come inside that Michigan and this property was where she would spend the rest of her life — Rottman began to shape her thoughts and words into a cohesive whole. "All Nature Sings: A Spiritual Journal of Place" is the result.

She decided about four years ago to create a book, so began gathering her journal entries, essays and thoughts. She structured it by month so readers, beginning in the unlikely month of November, can follow the land as it sleeps, then awakens and bursts into bloom, then sleeps again. She edited the book in real time, testing whether her observations coincided with what was actually happening around her.

"All Nature Sings" is a thoughtful, beautifully written cycle of growth and rest, life and death, spiritual questions and a few answers. Rottman's writing is smooth, her descriptions perceptive, her eye true. "Place is what holds it all

and take out my journal and try to relay all the things that were surprising to me."

After years

Carol Rottman

together, I'm hanging on to this piece of land, which has become my place and I've fallen in love with it," said Rottman.

No two chapters are the same — some contain hymns, poetry, essays, journal entries — though all contain photographs by Fritz Rottman and a final piece titled Environmental Notes that offers information on Rottman's chapter subjects and pertinent resources such as books and websites.

"I had no idea I was so rooted in things that grow and move and change and are all around me," said

Rottman. "I ignored a lot o that before this. It's a matte of slowing my pace a bit, of be ing a lot more open eyed an open eared."

Rottman says that the ne phase of their land stewa ship is sharing what th have done. Calvin College ology students help care the land as well as stud flowers, bogs, fish wildlife.

"This is wild land," she "This is not a place you h watch where you step."

Sharing the land: Carol Rottman's walks on her land northeast of Grand Rapids taught her to pay attention to changes in wildlife and plants. Among the creatures she sees are a downy woodpecker, left, and the beaver whose tail is seen in the photo below.

PHOTOS COURTESY
FRITZ ROTTMAN

E-mail: yourlife@grpress.co

ANNIVERSARIES

Emil and Esther Schulz

Emil and Esther (Halpen) Schulz of Caledonia will celebrate 70 years of marriage today, June 20. A lakeside dinner at their home on Duncan Lake will be held in honor of the occasion. Children of the couple are Lois Purtell Myers and Tom Myers, and Richard Schulz. They have one granddaughter.

Don and Shirley Schrotenboer

Fifty years of wedded life were observed June 16 by Don and Shirley (De Young) Schrotenboer of Holland. A family dinner will be held in honor of the occasion. Children of the couple are Rich and Lisa Schrotenboer and Dr. Greg and Diane Schrotenboer. They have six grandchildren.

Lawrence and Dorothy Scheidel

Sixty-five years as husband and wife will be observed today, June 20, by Lawrence and Dorothy (McKercher) Scheidel of Wayland. An open house will be held today from 2 to 5 p.m. at the home of their daughter and son-in-law, Karen and Bob Wiersma. The Scheidels'

other children are Ed and Suzanne Scheidel, Diane and Bob DeHaan, Char and Tom Sanok, Morris and Carol Scheidel, and Marty and Traci Scheidel. They have 27 grandchildren, 42 great-grandchildren and one great-great-granddaughter.

Leon and Sharon Talsma

Leon and Sharon (Nelson) Talsma of Wyoming will celebrate 50 years of marriage today, June 20. A trip to Camp Pendleton, Calif., to visit the wedding chapel where they were married will take place.

Patrick and Tina Talsma,

Russell and Lorraine Spooner

Seventy-five years of matrimony were observed June 16 by Russell and Lorraine (Leinum) Spooner of Grand Rapids. A family dinner was held in honor

Judy Spooner. They have

ext
d-
ey
bi-
for
its
and

said.
ave to

Natural Resources and in exchange for creating some feed-plots for ground birds, he seeded the fields with a mixture of wildflowers and native grasses. In much the same way that radiation had stopped his cancer, the five-year process of discouraging (if not eliminating) invasive plants stimulated natural or native growth. Each year the growth clumps have become fuller, just like our nurtured perennials nearer the house. Many pesky invasive plants, such as purple vetch and wild mustard, must be pulled or chopped by hand; it isn't easy to get rid of plants that have long enjoyed this land as though it were their own. Somewhere along the way I became the "weed spotter" and Fritz's pulling partner.

Next spring we must do the unthinkable: burn last year's dry grasses and stalks (see "April"). When the conditions are just right, we'll set fire to parts of the field, section by section, with the help of experienced burners. For a while, I'm told, the land will look like what remains after the scourge of a forest fire. But as the Native Americans knew long ago, native plants have deeper roots than weeds and will survive. I know that, as I walk the driveway after the burn, I'll have to look up at the clouds instead of down over the land, or the sight of the charred stubble could overwhelm me.

Then, even before there is any evidence of green poking upward, I'll have to believe that this death by frost, as well as by fire, will bring forth abundant new life. Just like Easter. In winter or on Good Friday or on my lowest days, renewal is hard to imagine. But God has a resurrection plan.

The seasons change. After long winters of quiet rebirth and the purposeful fire of the remaining stubble come seedtime and the promise of harvest. The groaning earth waits for just the right time to deliver a prairie full of wildflowers and waving grasses.

And I find myself convinced: *"LORD, you have assigned me my portion and my cup; you have made my lot secure. The boundary lines have fallen for me in pleasant places; surely I have a delightful inheritance."* (Psalm 16:5–6)

November, 2002
Sunday Dinner at Grandma's House

"Ready or not, here they come," I think as I walk in the back door and check the meat and vegetable dishes in the oven, thankful that the auto-start didn't fail me. No time to change out of church clothes as four vehicles unload children, their parents, great-aunt Mary and great-grandmother Casey. Fritz opens the front door, and the house comes to life, ready to receive eighteen hungry people for Sunday dinner.

Allow me to introduce: Firstborn Barb married Dave and produced Lindsay and Matt. Our middle child, Doug, married Mary and brought twins, Brian and Marielle, and then Morgan into the world. The baby of our family, Sue, married Steve and has three: Chris, Tori, and Dani. By some divine happenstance each kid, except for Lindsay, who is the eldest by five years, has a cousin of about his or her own age and gender.

The three boys, Matt, Chris, and Brian, hang together. Marielle and Tori, only a year apart, are best friends and even go to camp together in the summer. And then, so nicely timed, the youngest two are girls born only four months apart.

The kids, some carrying a bag of "must take" toys from home, offer hugs all around before disappearing with their cousins to the library, to our bedroom with its game drawer, or to the basement playroom. Even the two-year-old girls, Dani and Morgan, are sliding down the stairs to join the big kids in play. "Let the wild rumpus begin!" the eight wild things seem to say. Now and then a runner comes up to report, "The boys said 'no girls allowed' in their fort, and that really hurt our feelings!" Some wise adult responds, "No tattling—work it out."

In the kitchen the more mature group munches on chips and salsa or cheese and crackers while Grandpa cuts the ham and I arrange the garlic mashed potatoes, green bean casserole and salads on the buffet counter. "What's the occasion?" someone asks. "Early Thanksgiving?" To be honest, this grandma couldn't wait until the end of November to see everyone again.

We never call the troops until everything is ready—there are enough bodies already roaming through the kitchen, laughing and teasing, oblivious to the cooks' preparations. "Time to eat!" though, and they all come running. We join hands, making a very large circle. Our son suggests that we let the grandchildren pray by each thanking God for two things. They bless us all by their heartfelt words: "for food

and Jesus and cousins and being able to come to Grandpa and Grandma's house." We serve the children first and seat them at the elongated kitchen table, while most of the adults carry their plates to the quieter dining room.

"Grandma, this is the best chicken!" enthuses four-year-old Tori. Chris spots a pair of bluebirds flitting from the garden fence to gather their dinner from the garden floor. Marielle wonders whether Grandpa will be mad that they're in his garden. The last time we gathered en masse was for the August birthdays, so the kids begin to talk about the next cluster of birthdays in late January and February. Brian, a twin, announces that he doesn't want his sister to have his same birthday. There is a lively "pickle preference" discussion. When plates are pretty clean, the kids get to pass more homemade applesauce. They are excused before dessert of apple or pumpkin pie, preferring the trick-or-treat suckers Matt brought along for everyone.

This event, like others before, almost brings me to tears. As a child, I never knew a Sunday dinner at Grandma's house. All of my grandparents except for one grandfather had died before I was born. My parents were transplants from Western Michigan to Colorado, leaving their huge families (including all of my cousins) for a life out West. Our Sunday dinner table included our family of seven and any "stranger" Mom could find at church. Close friends of my parents became pseudo "aunts" and "uncles," but their children were not considered cousins. There were good times, to be sure, but not at Grandma's house.

My four siblings and I scattered after high school, eventually settling in different states; later on Mom and Dad took a traveling job that took them all over the United States. Because Fritz and I longed for a close grandparent relationship for our own children, we planted our first roots in East Lansing, about two hours from Muskegon, so we could occasionally share Sunday dinner with his parents. Our kids remember haunts like clothes closets, the attic, Grandpa's shed and the long, narrow backyard they shared with cousins on Sunday afternoons. And they remember Grandma's roast beef.

I never even dared to hope that we could regularly reenact those kinds of family gatherings. We reasoned that our children should not be bound by our need for their presence. We raised them for leaving, just as our parents had done with us. So I am amazed today to find myself amidst all of our children and grandchildren, and even one sister and my mother, gathered in one place, on a Sunday afternoon. Wild but wonderful!

By some stroke of non-planning, Lindsay, nicknamed "Queenie" because she had eight adults fawning over her before the other kids were born, knows how to create games out of chaos. But today one loud bang and a scream from the basement interrupt our adult conversation. "Matt hit his head on the table, and he's bleeding bad," the messenger announces. Not to worry; we have a doctor and a nurse among us to staunch the bleeding and assess the damage. "A few stitches would help the healing—but no hurry." Nine-year-old Matt goes back to rough play, proud to be getting more stitches to add to his lifetime record of twenty-seven.

It's a balmy day for November, so after yesterday's puddles dry a bit, most of the kids head out. It's past time to pick red raspberries or carrots in the garden, and the lake no longer beckons us to fish or swim, but there are still earthworms and wooly caterpillars to discover. I "ooh" and "aah" over a brown creature balled in my hand but decline the save him as my new pet.

If this sounds too good to be true, listen more closely. The siblings are still rivals at times, they don't always share our political views, my sons-in-law love to tease me, and I have sometimes wished I were free to spank a kid or two. Just underneath the surface are the typical concerns of young families, and over us all hovers the uncertainty of our times. But today we rest in togetherness.

Our story in retirement is becoming more common. After eighteen years in Cleveland we decided to relocate near our children, who all, for a variety of reasons, have settled in this area. So we found land and built in the country, less than an hour from the three families, just far enough away to make Sunday dinner an event and days like this a rare wonder. It would be easy to idolize family and try to repeat this togetherness every Sunday, but our usual guests are the strangers my mother has taught me to welcome. The rare Sunday dinner at Grandma's house makes it all the more precious.

As four cars finally pull away down the drive, I add my prayer to that of the children: "Thanks for a Sabbath blessing. Thanks for a glimpse of Shalom."

Carpet of Leaves

The Silhouette Season

Bright colors of dancing flame fade to embers
when leaves announce the finale
of the growing, mellow-warm, life-giving season
and let go, spinning and drifting down.

Layers of gorgeous debris delight us
with crackle and crunch in a patchwork
of startling color—a crazy, changing quilt
we want to hold from turning a monotone brown.

Saved leaves delight, then curl, all spotted brittle
in the trash. Last holdouts of oak and willow
finally join the forest's carpet, blending
gold and crimson in a hearty winter soup.

At first light or day's last glow the naked trees stand
unashamed in the distance, without costume or
curtain. Not even a fig leaf hides their skinny
shaking limbs, reaching desperately heavenward.

Crayon art rounds branches with mandatory leaves,
supplying what no longer hangs, as if a
tree is not a tree without its clothes. But life buds
inside, growing a ringed mark in winter's dark chill.

The silhouette season—melancholy, brooding, lonely—
a colorless contrast of beautifully bleak timber,
in the vast shadowbox of life: completely awake,
stoking the fire-glow within.

C. Rottman, 2000

Before the westward movement of civilization in North American, millions of acres of tallgrass prairies dominated

the land. But by the 1900s prairies of the Midwest were on the brink of destruction, mainly because of the use of the steel plow that opened the land for farming and development. Now a new wave of "restoration pioneers" in the Plains work to

Tallgrass Prairie Indian Grass

reclaim some of this vital habitat for native grasses, forbs (some of which are wildflowers) and animal life.

Prairie restoration has grown into a movement among land conservationists, small landowners and gardeners. In some states, the Division of Natural Resources will help plant and share the cost of the seeds. In addition to the natural beauty such projects promote, the tall grasses, with their deep root structures and minimal demand for water, aid conservation of topsoil and deter erosion. Prairie flowers attract pollinators, such as butterflies and bees, and thus enhance fruit and vegetable growth. Once a prairie is established, it thrives with little maintenance, while enriching both the earth and the living things dwelling within its bounds.

Lady Bird Johnson, remembered as our environmental First Lady, raised cultural awareness of beautification with wildflowers. She promoted the Beautification Act of 1965 that generated funds for planting wildflowers along public highways. The Surface Transportation and Uniform Relocation Assistance Act of 1987 requires that at least a quarter of one-percent of funds expended for landscaping projects in the highway system be used to plant native flowers, plants and trees. Because of Lady Bird Johnson's efforts, we see wildflowers blooming along the nation's highways, as well as fewer junkyards and billboards.

The Johnson administration was the most active in conservation since the Roosevelt era, largely due to the efforts of Mrs. Johnson. A total of 200 pieces of legislation relevant to the environment were enacted during those years, including the Wilderness Act of 1964, along with the inception of the Land and Water Conservation Fund and the Wild and Scenic Rivers Program. But the multi-colored, waving wildflowers along highways and byways remain her lasting legacy.

Learn more:
www.wildflowers.org
Restoring the Tallgrass Prairie by Shirley Shirley

Christmas is coming.

The geese are getting fat.

Please put a penny in the old man's hat.

If you haven't got a penny, a half-penny will do.

If you haven't got a half-penny,

God Bless You.

Frozen Stalks

All Nature Sings: A Spiritual Journey of Place

December means hunkering down for winter. The naked trees, silhouetted against the pale sky, creak in the wind, with snow clinging to their north sides. Several light snow squalls have scattered a little powder, but we have yet to see measurable amounts that bend and mat the tall grasses toward the earth. Yesterday the wind blew so powerfully across the lake that whitecaps formed. Our garden looks like a menagerie of plant skeletons with a few green rows of winter rye, used to hold and enrich the soil for next year. From the warmth of indoors, we watch the sun rise brilliantly through layers of clouds and the birds happily scratching for seeds in their feeders. We hunker down to our deskwork, but it seems at first like all work and no play. We brace ourselves for months of indoor recess. Day's end comes before we are ready, as the sun goes down early on the other side of the house. The black trees stand in sharp contrast to the majestic, multicolored sunset.

You will go out in joy and be led forth in peace; the mountains and hills will burst into song before you, and all the trees of the field will clap their hands.

(Isaiah 55:12)

Both of us seek shelter from the harsh weather in our little hollows, like so many of the hibernating animals. Although we don't store up enough food in our bodies for the winter, we do live off the sensory fuel we've stored. My den is an upstairs room with three windows on the peaked north wall, which let in as much light as the day affords. My desk faces the east wall, devoid of light and the distraction of nature. Even with the Van Gogh print "Peach Blossoms in the Crau" facing me, I can lose myself in my work. I have finally gotten used to the hum of my computer, but, unfortunately, my room can be too warm in summer and too cold in winter, so a rattling heater/cooler unit is often my companion here. When I'm on a roll, neither temperature nor noise matters. When I'm stuck, I have something to blame.

Fritz's den is on the lower level, with his desk facing the open field and the lake beyond. He doesn't mind the outside stimulation and often calls up to me when he spies something of interest. During the summertime, on one day it was the swans trying to teach their young one to fly. On another he spied a beaver swimming past, leaving a broad, v-shaped wake. On days when I get no call but hear some shouting below, I know the extended family of geese is pooping on the dock again. Because two flights of stairs separate us, we often e-mail each other. We could just as well be at separate offices away from home, as we were for most of our married lives. But now we always meet for lunch.

I live in a perpetual retreat, especially in wintertime. How could I have known that this particular spot on God's good Earth would be a place just right for me? Even though I worked for years to create a "writing life" so that my post-work days would remain full of meaning and activity, I had thought more about what I'd be doing than where I'd be doing it. I had assumed I could write anywhere. Yet except for my daily walks to the mailbox, I hate to leave my retreat. If I lived in the city, I might be pulled by one activity after another. I'd hop in my car and run to the store for this and that and meet friends for lunch. There are already enough distractions in my own mind—I don't need others. Trips to town are preplanned and activities clustered so that most of my time is spent right here. Other writers talk of taking a writing residency; mine is right here. And winter is primetime.

December always comes too early

I'm never ready for the last of the beech leaves to fade or fall or for the oak leaves to shrivel and turn brown. The silhouette season always arrives on schedule. A certain finality to the sensory announcement shouts: Winter is here. In climates like ours in Michigan—where the winter looms long—we have to wait at least four months until hints appear that change is coming. Only a few months ago, during a church service, we sang to the accompaniment of clapping and drums, "Come all you people, come and praise your Maker; come now and worship the Lord." It's easier to be exuberant over creation when you're warm and when you can pick fresh beans for dinner and see yellow blooms waving across the fields. In winter, God seems to go into hiding.

Just when I've accepted the jacket season, it comes time for boots, a muffler and an ear-covering hat. There is no wind-break along the drive. When I'm bundled against the icy winds that sweep across the fields, my eyes are downcast, looking for frozen puddles that could catch me off guard. Careful as I am, a patch of ice invariably catches me unawares, my feet slip out from under me, and in seconds I'm flat on my back checking to see whether anything is broken. Immediately another line of thinking sets in: What will I have to give up if I'm laid up? As I get up and brush myself off, I wonder whether these walks to the mailbox are really worth it. But I could as easily slip getting out of the car. Walking the length of the driveway, I'm on my guard. I don't want the fear of falling, or any other kind of fear, to immobilize me. Fear that something might happen is nearly always worse than the actual occurrence; fear relies on imagining the worst-case scenario. So I'll take precautions but won't stay indoors—unless I really break a leg.

Some ice is nice. Flat Iron Lake freezes solid when the temps remain consistently below freezing for a string of days, usually in late November or December. We've had some of our best times ice-skating down there when the lake freezes quickly and leaves a smooth surface before the snow falls. If enough kids come, they clear a whole hockey rink. When I come down with my skates over my shoulder, the kids seem surprised that Grandma still likes to skate. Growing up in Colorado, my friends and I skated in the city park and on mountain lakes.

The first snow usually comes in December, amid a flurry of fanfare by the forecasters. It's often moderate but a good reminder to check the tread on the tires and return the ice scraper to the car. Because of the distances and the rural roads, we also put some emergency clothing in the trunk and religiously carry the mobile phone. Winter or not, snacks fill the console between the seats, just in case. I wonder whether I could ever parcel these bars out over days, as I've heard folks have had to do when marooned. We are ready for winter driving, but I look for every excuse to stay home, where the refrig is stocked and the garden fare we stored in the freezer is at the ready. Fritz gets the generator ready and makes sure there's a supply of wood in case the electricity goes out when ice weighs down the power lines. We think we're prepared, but when it happens we are totally disoriented for hours, learning anew how to manage without our usual gadgets and comforts.

We use our wood-burning stove in the basement only when the power goes out, which is quite often out here. But

Frozen Flat Iron Lake

I know what it takes to stoke it, as we used to do in the wood stove in Colorado. As long as there are some live embers, the fire can be revived. The embers need air and fuel to keep the fire-glow alive. When it's almost out, I add a little kindling and blow gently until a flame fans from underneath.

My writing life could be likened to wood in a stove. God's Spirit must be the breath blowing life onto my work. God created this desire in me and doesn't want it to go from smolder to cold. Writing is also like nature in winter. God didn't make living things, whether beasts or blooms, to thrive only in the pleasant growing seasons. "Maker and Sustainer" are two parts of God's role—he lights the fire and keeps it going, plants a tree and stays with it through winter's chill, until it flowers once again. Seeds and hibernating animals bide their time to emerge from the cold.

Occasionally Fritz cuts fallen trees with a chain saw, in lengths that, when split, will fit into the bed of the stove. The sharp, crosswise cuts reveal the growth rings of the tree. We can tell the age of the tree by the number of rings; spaces between rings show how much growth occurred. In December we inevitably look back over the past year. I wish I had internal rings to give an indisputable mark of a year of growth. Was it a full, productive growing season for me? Hopefully I gained some stature and girth of understanding.

Where in the world is Carmen San Diego?

"Where in Michigan is this tract of land you call home?" asked my teacher at a workshop after reading my first chapter, "November." Good question, I thought. When reading almost any story on the WEB news, a little box appears with a funny arrow pointing to a location on the map. I'd been so busy writing the text, I'd forgotten the context. Where in the world is Flat Iron Lake?

That same aerial view we now know as Google Earth can be broadened to show where our land is situated in the greater scheme of things. Hart Street is a short, east-west road between two north-south roads, Wabasis and Lincoln Lake, both owing their names to other lakes. The whole area is spotted with inland lakes, many within a short bike ride of Flat Iron. We are situated in Western Michigan, about fifteen miles north of Grand Rapids, the second largest city in the state after Detroit. East and West Michigan are often worlds apart politically, religiously and culturally, with both Michigan and Michigan State Universities located as buffers in between.

Our rural mailbox delivery comes from Greenville, but our place is halfway between it and Rockford on the west. We identify with neither town, which may say a lot about our feelings of peaceful isolation. North of us the wildness of the lower peninsula of Michigan increases along Highway 131, until it reaches the Mackinac Bridge and the Upper Peninsula. To the west, one has the choice of lovely, white-sand beaches along the coast of Lake Michigan. Because of Fritz's roots in Muskegon, a lake port, we regularly went to a family cottage nearby.

On days when I wonder about the deep-seated love of water on the part of the people around me, I have only to close my eyes and listen to the waves lapping along the shoreline as the sun sets over the Big Lake, as Michiganders are wont to call it. Where in the world? Somewhere near water. I know the longing, although it's mountains, not water, that always tug at my heartstrings. Landscape subtly shapes us.

The Experiment

Neither prior knowledge nor expertise prepared us for living on this land. Fritz was in the league, with his early curiosity about living things and immersion in the life sciences, but he'd be the first to admit that he knew little about prairies and what it would take to bring back native growth after decades of other uses of the land. My ignorance of the ways of nature drove me back into the kids' section of the library for some elementary facts.

I grew up in the city, and although my dad dabbled in gardening because of his own rural roots, I knew little about it and cared even less. I recall being assigned to rescue overgrown strawberries and beans after the gardener had gotten too busy to notice. No pet lasted long in our home. The only animals I saw were the dozen chickens Dad once received in payment for medical services—soon butchered. Several puppies ripped things up before being outplaced with other families. Fritz and I, in contrast, have rarely been without a dog in the house and a vegetable garden nearby.

I'm still amazed that either of us launched this prairie experiment with so little forethought. Fritz's scientific mind and eye for natural beauty got us into this; I was naively open to its possibilities but never thought of myself as a partner. As the years pass, I try to recollect when I became active, not only in the work but also in the wonder of it all. When did this place attach itself to me like a burr that couldn't be shaken off my clothing? My love seemed to grow like the plants—small during the first year and larger and fuller each year thereafter. Now my roots are deep. I want to drop seeds everywhere.

Advent

Just when we are prone to gaze backward, the Christian calendar forces us to look ahead. In this part of the world—northern Midwest—we can certainly anticipate four to five months of cold, often disagreeable weather. But late November or early December also brings the season of Advent, a time for anticipation of Christ's coming.

Advent: The Word becoming flesh and moving right in with us. You'd think, after all these years of reminders to get ready, that we'd be prepared—permanently. But no. We can't even imagine what it would be like if Jesus were to come and live in our neighborhood or on our prairie. We would be forced to watch how we spent our time. We'd check whether or not our front door was open to the alien and the stranger or only to people we already knew. We know we'd have to change: to begin thinking more about others than ourselves. When the kids were small, I used to sing little ditties to them. After hearing the first Salvation Army bell in the mall and dropping coins into the bucket, this old English song made some sense:

Christmas is coming.
The geese are getting fat.

Please put a penny in the old man's hat.
If you haven't got a penny, a half-penny will do.
If you haven't got a half-penny,
God Bless You.

We've all got more pennies now, and the hat is still outstretched. We shouldn't have to wait for his coming at Christmas or until the coming of the new heaven and the new Earth to know how to use all those pennies. But early Christmas ads beg us to spend our pennies and dollars on our family or our selves. Paul Mariani confessed in *Thirty Days: On Retreat* about "the thick, bittersweet molasses of money... this greenback demon, lurking in the thickets there. This one surprised me by masquerading as concern for my family."

Need is everywhere. The red kettle bell rings out the question: Which old beggar's hat will you fill this season?

Holiday Greetings

The trek to the mailbox gets more interesting in December, even as the snow piles up. The white landscape is dotted with mellow brown stalks of tall grasses hearty enough to stand or bow under the blanket covering them. On the rare sunny day, the reflection of light from the snow nearly blinds me; fortunately, I know the way. Waiting for me now, instead of a nearly empty mailbox, stands the green plastic box stuffed with catalogs, pleas for charitable contributions (a version of

the old man's hat) and many hand-addressed envelopes bringing holiday greetings from friends.

Each type of mail comes with its own imperative: buy, give or write back. Most of the catalogs go into the recycle box, the pleas for money on a pile for year-end decisions but the Christmas letters seem to blare an awful reminder: it is time to write yours. Each year we consider a different way to keep in touch with friends until the long list and the short amount of time convince us that a group letter is the only way forward.

Since I am the designated scribe in the family, I begin, but with the stern warning that mine is only a draft to be edited. As we dither over what to say and how to say it, other Christmas letters arrive, making the job even more difficult. Writing used to be easy when the news was really news, that of a new baby or a new job or a change of address. But now when we get a letter from a long-lost friend that is really over-the-top, it feels like a stern warning not to fall into that trap. After all, our kids are not all geniuses, our travels not more spectacular or newsworthy than those of others and our opinions—really ours alone. So what DO we write?

The December pleasure of hearing from friends becomes a burden. I could write a whole book in the time it takes to fashion one letter acceptable to both of us. Mine usually begin with a little flare of insight or observation and goes on to the family happenings. But since there are now so many units in our greater family, I must consider how my pen describes another family's news. Before long what I thought was news is removed because it is too something: braggy, arty, dull, or insignificant. By the time this letter is sanitized and homogenized it is more like those skeletons of plants that dot last year's garden: lifeless, drained of color, frozen in time.

With the advent of digital cameras and easier import of pictures into text, small photographs can supply what excised words cannot. The reader/viewer can form his own impressions. Perhaps that could be a plan for next year's letter. Just pictures with carefully selected captions; you, reader, fill in the blanks.

Finally, with just enough time for a December 24th delivery, I carry our bundle of cards with letters tucked inside back out to the rural mailbox and raise the red flag. No more second guessing about message or implied meaning—until next year.

Walking back to the house along the snow-covered drive, I see clearer images all around of simple beauty. Memory supplies the color and scents that are dormant. I wonder if these every day bits of news can ever be put into a holiday letter.

The Gifts We Don't Expect

The kids I know best have no problem with December: Cold and snow excite, Christmas looms, and holiday baking for parties and school events invites participation. The advent calendar and the Christmas pageant and carols wrestle their attention toward Christ's birth and away from preoccupation of gifts—their own—for a while.

However, I remember the sparkling eyes of each of my children as they opened those first gifts. A box carrying his or her name, covered with paper and sealed with a bow until some adult gave the signal that the time of waiting was over. When I was young, the Santa myth was firmly squelched, so that we were allowed to open our presents on Christmas Eve after we got back from the Sunday School program. Sometimes Dad made us read the Christmas story one more time to ensure that we'd keep the "true meaning" front and center: "And so it was, that, while they were there, the days were accomplished that she should be delivered. And she brought forth her firstborn son…." (Luke 2:6–7 KJV) God's best gift to us! Dad reminded us before we ripped the covering off our gifts. At times we were so excited we forgot to thank the giver.

The same scene repeats itself at our current family Christmas gatherings. At first the kids were all about getting gifts, but gradually that morphed into excitement about giving the gifts they had selected for a cousin and watching his amazement when he tore open the wrappings. But it's still a stretch for me to make the conversion: Because Christ gave his all for me, including coming as a babe, I should be about giving to others.

No one ever suggested that this land I now occupy was a gift just for me, but as I begin to write about my pilgrimage here, I recognize that this is exactly what it is. Not only is it

God's gracious gift; it is also the frame within which I have an opportunity to see "his glory... full of grace and truth." (John 1:14) The chance is here, but as with all gifts, I must receive it, take it in, and incorporate it as part of myself.

At first I might have said what I thought: Flat Iron Lake is not on my wish list. I anticipated a different sort of home base—a return to the mountains of my birth. I had spent much of my life longing for it—a longing refueled each year by our return to that old house in Marble, Colorado, and then by an extended sabbatical in Boulder.

Flat Iron Lake is my consolation gift. I think back to one Christmas of my childhood when I was hoping for a new doll but opened a package to find only doll clothes for the old one. I tried to mask my disappointment. But later on, as I played with my familiar doll and finally let the phantom wish fly away, I discovered that I was left holding just what I had wanted.

"Curiosity was my saving grace. I followed my grandchildren and saw things through their eyes."

To say that I was unprepared for this gift of place is painfully true—I couldn't even imagine a use for it. I never took a serious biology or botany course or worked at a summer camp—and I only watched my green-thumb husband plant and tend his gardens and trees. I had to start at the beginning, like a child, seeing, hearing and sensing the world around me as though for the first time—which it often was. Picking and cooking had been my job, and for that I didn't have to understand what preceded the fruit on the vine.

Curiosity was my saving grace. I followed my grandchildren and saw things through their eyes. With each sighting in each season my list of questions grew. The closer I looked, the more mysterious things caught my eye. Books, the Internet, Fritz and even the kids themselves became my teachers. I needed them all.

What I saw was and is glorious—in fact, I sense God everywhere. Sometimes he feels like my little brother, always tagging along; sometimes like the scouting guide who knows the safest way to go. I always have lots of questions for him, too—mostly "why" questions. Why am I here—in this world and on this acreage? Why did God pick this gift to bring me to an understanding of his work and ways? Why am I being asked to write about it? Curiosity is also killing me, but I have to trust that someday God will place every last piece in all of these puzzles.

Advent reminds me: Christ is coming. God with us, Immanuel. The One who will make all things plain.

Oak Tree in Winter

One morning a few oak leaves from the big old trees along the lake blew onto the driveway. Rusty brown on black asphalt makes for striking contrast. I catch one and examine it, realizing that it differs from other oak leaves near the house. This one is flat and broad, and the other has deeper cuts and still hangs onto the tree. I share my observations with Fritz and soon learn that "we" planted four varieties of oak on the outside rim of the drive. The closer I look, with the help of his naturalist eye, the more differences I see in the bark, arrangement of the branches and types of acorns. I thought I was making progress by distinguishing an oak from a maple, but now I'll have to look deeper than the superficial differences to sub-types of the same species. And as I learn the variations within a type, I'll begin to see and appreciate each tree more.

My reaction to oak trees is like prejudice; so often I lump people or ideas that are different or "other" into one ball. An overall category gives only one unifying principle, when really humans may have as much in common with people of a different race or political persuasion as trees with different leaves and bark have within their type. At first glance, the features of faces and the colors of leaves seem so uniform that I hardly see their particularity. Close examination reveals a plethora of exciting variation. Not until I get to know another person and her ideas do her particular qualities become notable. Trees teach me to look beyond large groups to smaller and smaller subgroups and then to individuals, each precious in its own right.

Jake's nose propels him from one clump of bushes to the woodpile and down to the lake. His nose tells him that animals, large and small, lurk nearby. If we are out early enough, he might scare up some nesting deer that were completely hidden from me. As I strain to see them bound all the way to the woods, I'm surprised that something that large could lie only a few feet away and yet be so completely camouflaged.

But when snow falls during the night, even just a light dusting, I find evidence of wildlife surrounding me by the footprints they have left behind. Not only do the prints reveal who was there but also which direction he or she was headed. I could follow the tracks and look for them, but don't. It's hard enough for me to recognize them by species. The cat-like paws are the hardest to identify from memory, but I imagine wild cats or foxes when they are probably only barn cats. Rabbit tracks with their larger and longer back feet are easy to spot. There are no small bunny tracks, so I know the multitudes of babies we saw in the spring have either succumbed or matured, which is a scary thought. The cloven hooves of deer crisscross the driveway—they're continually heading toward the woods for better cover, especially during hunting season.

Several times I've seen the three-pronged track of a pheasant. They have a hard time surviving because of the predators, but their little fan-feet tell me they were here. Miniature tracks fascinate me. The mouse-like vole that I rarely see in daylight leave their marks, kind of like a drunken sailor. And then a mystery track—so small it could be that of an insect. I pull my scarf higher on my neck against the cold and wonder where and how these creatures stay warm.

Soon Jake's big paws and the nails he uses for traction corrupt the animal road map on the new-fallen snow. And here are my size ten clogs with characteristic tread, starting and stopping on no more of a straight a line than the roaming animals that were here just moments earlier. Later, while eating breakfast and looking in the animal field guide, I wonder whether the hidden creatures are now examining our tracks, trying to discover who we are and where we are going. Hey, guys, when you figure that out—I'd like to know.

JOURNAL ENTRY

December 25, 2004–Christmas morning! Earlier this morning I walked Jake in the cold, crisp world, wearing my new, long, cranberry-colored robe—a gift from Fritz. I was cozy walking down the driveway—as I do each day—to observe the sights and sounds around Flat Iron Lake. Today the sky was an overcast gray and last night's full moon completely hidden. The roosters from across the lake were in competition once again for rights to declare that morning had broken. Jake must smell something right under the snow's surface, for he puts his nose down, moves a few feet, and plunges his black nose again until he has to come up for air. Yesterday he scared up two white-tail deer—the first we've seen for many days. They are as scarce for viewing as they have reportedly been for hunters this year. I love to watch their white butts bobbing up and down until they reach the forest cover.

Last night I stayed up to read a fascinating new book, Midnight Disease *(the neurobiology of hypergraphia—the compulsion to write). When I finally turned off all the lights, the scene was awesome. The full moon was out of sight but illuminating the snow on just the kind of night when kids might imagine a sleigh in the sky. From my bedroom window I could see a star—no imagining—brightly shining over the place, somewhere in time and space, where Jesus lay.*

New Year's Eve Celebration

MEDITATION

"The Word became flesh and made his dwelling among us." (John 1:14)

One of my friends does not celebrate Christmas. He does not mark time, as I do, by the church calendar—by a new Lectionary year, with the first four Sundays building anticipation of Christ's incarnation. Instead, he marks a turning point on the day in December known as the Winter Solstice. The day is at the same time an end and a beginning, the moment from which days stop getting shorter and start getting longer—not with more time overall, but just with more possible daylight.

A turning point, like the solstice or Christmas, can also be a climax—the point at which the action in a story changes direction. The fleeting moment in time marking the ends and the beginnings of years have also been for me such a moment. When that glowing ball falls precisely at midnight in Times Square, everyone cheers. The hope always remains that this time, this moment, this year, our story can begin again.

Animals in wintertime teach us many things about survival in the cold. At Flat Iron Lake some creatures have demonstrated their ability to conserve heat and survive the freezing temps of lake and land. Spring peepers and their friends, the chorus frogs and gray treefrogs, make the first sounds heralding spring when the ice breaks up in the swale. Where were they all winter? We have learned that when one of these frogs feels the first frost on its skin, that stress triggers a quick rise in blood glucose that acts like antifreeze for its cells. Frogs become frozen solid, except for the insides of their cells. Each frog's heart stops, no blood flows, and it no longer breathes. Its body waits for the first flush of spring. When it wakes up, along with its frog cousins, it sings wildly to attract a mate.

Beavers, our largest rodent, do not hibernate but live in a carefully constructed stick- and mud-insulated lodge. Their home is a two-story mound rising as high as seven feet, with an air vent on top. The beaver family enters from below through a water seal at the base of the lodge and then spends up to six months huddled together in total darkness during winter, feeding on caches of cut branches or eating only the few plants it finds underwater in order to stay alive. If the water seal does not stay submerged, the lodge is ruined, and they must build a new home before winter comes again. Maybe that's the reason they want to keep the water level high by making dams.

Squirrels hide nuts, birds puff out their feathers, and garter snakes shun their singular ways and huddle together, like a mass of spaghetti. Field mice try to get into our warm houses and garages, but if that fails they build underground tunnels that act like geo-thermal heating systems. Bees expend as little energy as possible and feed off the honey they've put away into the hive (minus what we harvest).

What have we learned from the animals? When the weather turns cold, we humans wear more layered clothing to conserve body heat, play active winter sports, or stay indoors by the fire. Our antifreeze goes into the radiator of the car, not into our cells; we seal our windows against the drafts; our less active bodies consume less food for fuel (if we're smart); and we snuggle closer to one another. We are learning more ways to conserve: insulation, dialing down the furnace and using energy-efficient light bulbs. We could follow the animals' example and eat locally grown food, like root vegetables from Michigan cellars and carrots buried below the frost line. And it would not hurt us to get plenty of rest. When spring comes, perhaps we will all wake up singing—ready for a new season of work.

Learn more:

Animal, Vegetable, Miracle: A Year of Food Life
by Barbara Kingsolver
Winter World: The Ingenuity of Animal Survival
by Bernd Heinrich

A new string of days stretches out as they have in my life

for almost three-score and ten.

An undefined hope seems to glow at the dawn of the

New Year... Outdoors I see covering of snow, under sunshine,

which accentuates its brilliant effect.

Winter's Brilliance

January reminds me of mortality. A new year-of-days stretches out as it has in my life for almost seventy years. At the dawn of the year, as I put away the Christmas ornaments, an undefined hope seems to glow. I hang up a new calendar with its bright images on twelve pages, each appropriate to the seasons in this part of the world. So many days ahead—surely this year I will use them wisely, make better decisions, and never put off for tomorrow what can be done today. But these days, like others before them, with all of their hope of change, seem to tumble by like dry weeds. Even as the year begins, I'm confronted by the futility of trying to catch them and hang on.

Days are like grass or weeds—but they are also like snow. Outdoors, I see a new covering of the white stuff under sunshine, accentuating the brilliant effect. Dried grasses and flower stalks bend over under the weight, leaving bumps that in certain light remind me of waves on a blue lake. Snow covers much of winter's dullness here on the prairie in the same way as it makes picture postcards of abandoned, crumbling farmhouses. The cover of snow is as deceptive as that calendar of pages; one unseasonably warm day melts beauty to slush and then to mud. Days pass, whether or not we want them to, and we know that all our days will eventually be used up. My walk through a year of days in this book helps me savor them, knowing full well that they are numbered.

One of Fritz's favorite pieces of music is Vivaldi's *The Four Seasons*. The seed catalogs always follow on the heels of Christmas catalogs, and he pores over them like a kid. Despite what he sees outside, the glossy, colored pages help him visualize the next crop of acorn squash and beefsteak tomatoes. Some of our friends seek warmer places in winter, but we usually stay put, in order to be a part of the unfolding drama that is the change of seasons. We can't reject our surroundings just because we're shivering and they're hidden under ice and snow. So we don't join the "snowbirds" and head south. We can't quite abandon the real winter snowbirds.

Fritz feels that it's his winter calling to "feed the birds," albeit with lots less flair than Mary Poppins, singing and dancing through hoards of pigeons in London. While I figure we can't possibly feed the multitudes of finches, let alone woodpeckers, chickadees and cardinals around Flat Iron Lake, he laments that he has somehow failed them when the birdfeeders go empty. "It's so cold," he says after filling the plastic cavities with birdseed. When several birds shivered and died right outside his office window, he blamed himself and vowed to watch the feeders more closely: "I know lots of birds die in the winter, but I just can't stand to watch it happen."

Somehow he doesn't place the same value on the life of a mouse, especially if it should decide to move in with us. Field mice should know how to survive the winter outside, he reasons, as he lays out traps where their telltale droppings are seen. I won't touch a mouse, much less look at them when dead, so it's all up to him. We should have kept a tally of all the unwanted guests that found themselves in the garbage can—quite dead. He keeps a concoction of peanut butter and soft cheese to re-bait the traps. It doesn't have to be this way. Rodent parents could warn their children about the dangers of living in people's houses, just as the deer warn theirs about electric fences.

Days with a Purpose

January can be a letdown after the rush-rush of the holidays. Again this year we made plans to use the first days of the New Year purposefully. As an antidote to the post-holiday blues, we scheduled our annual trip to volunteer in Africa only five days into the year. But on the first day of 2008, the political situation changed in Kenya following that country's national election. All of our plans dissolved. We followed the horrendous news reports and could only imagine the chaos following the contested results. News of bloodshed and live footage on television shocked us as political opposition turned deadly.

We were saddened that friends and people we do not yet know are living in constant danger in this once-model African country. As the tension continued in Kenya, we realized that we could not even reschedule our trip and reclaim our air tickets for another date. Associates in Kenya and Uganda urged us not to come, as the situation remained volatile and they could not assure our safety. Our trip was optional; their life there—required.

We were left with an empty feeling as we put away our warm-weather clothing and stowed the waiting suitcases in the basement storeroom. A cloud of sadness covered us too—our resiliency was tested even as we worried over them, almost ashamed to continue living in relative comfort and peace. We wondered how we could reclaim these days for good.

We needed a diversion from our constant preoccupation: "If we were in Africa now, we'd be in _____ doing _____ ." One day we remembered an offer to use someone's condo in Gulf Shores for a week. So we hurried south to Alabama and spent a week in a slightly warmer and sunnier place, one free from our usual distractions. We did something we'd never done before: sat day after day at a kitchen table just inches from each other and both wrote, Fritz tackling his memoirs for the first time. Amazingly, it worked—neither of us distracted the other.

Journal Entry

January, 2008—It's the last day of our week, and thoughts of home now supersede those of Africa. Home even trumps all the writing we're both doing here. I'm eager for the rhythm of days on Flat Iron Lake—the dog and I shuffling out into whatever weather has descended during the night; Fritz and I checking the news of the day over breakfast and then bidding farewell at the stairwell before he goes down and I go up to our respective desks to work. And then, when work is done or I've reached my mental or physical limit, I bundle up for the walk to the mailbox. Do I live for that walk? It certainly is a high point of the day—so much greater than any mail that might await me down the road.

Marking Time

The passing of time has always bothered me. I began to mark my days in new ways after my father died suddenly in his sleep in January—not in frigid Michigan but in Okla-homa City, where he was working. But we buried him in his homeland of Western Michigan on a weekend of one of those horrendous weather events that now seem almost commonplace. I cannot turn the January page until I revisit memories of my father.

His death was my first personal experience with mortality, in the loss of someone I loved. I never knew my grandparents, and living as we did in Colorado, I didn't know most of my aunts and uncles, my parents' twenty-one siblings, many of whom had died before I even heard their names. So the death of my dad at the age of only seventy came as a shock, but it also came at a time when I was already living in perpetual shock and grief. Six months earlier, our son Doug had been injured in an accident and was still in the hospital, unable to move anything below his shoulders. We had faced the possibility of the death of our child; miraculously, he lived, but his life was compromised.

So when the news came of Dad's heart attack and death, my fragile coping powers bowed beneath yet another weight, like heavy snow pushing me toward the ground. But death does not come conveniently—it just comes. We met our family members after a five-hour drive in awful weather to comfort each other and to lay our father to rest. My memory of those days is of someone pretending to be me, saying and doing the right things because I had no energy to grieve. In the tradition of our family, several siblings wrote tributes to Dad, and one read a psalm that seemed to speak of him. I was speechless. Later on I must have written this clumsy poem, which I recently found on yellow notepaper:

Fear fills me
  hands are wet,
  stomach tight
On the way to our unplanned reunion.

Change disturbs me;
  Dad is not here.
  Can we his children,
find ourselves united, around his death?

Hugs and tears
  give way to old joy in sharing
  stories past, alongside
this uncanny present—a broken circle of family.

Yesterdays shine clearer than today,
  Even as gifts are credited—
  debts acknowledged—
  to Dad, whose illusive presence
lives on in all our futures.

                    C. Rottman, 1982

After the funeral I shelved my grief—unable to revisit it. More than twenty years later I realized the folly of choosing not to do the difficult work of coming to terms with death. "Dad, whose illusive presence lives on in all our futures…" was something I'd written but never reckoned with. In fact, the sadness of losing him began smoldering into resentment—that he hadn't told us how dangerous his heart condition was, that he had smoked for most of his life, that he wouldn't stop working in favor of enjoying his grandchildren. But most of all, I harbored anger that he had never allowed me to get close to him, especially in his later years, even though we had so much in common and I revered him for inspiring me as a lover of language and written thought. I wanted to enjoy his beautiful mind, but it seemed as though he either would not or could not let me.

He left a hundred pages of memoir. Before I had tried my own hand at writing, I could never have begun to calculate what an effort those pages represented. Though his words were highly literate, they were impersonal—an assessment shared by my siblings. All those years ago, when I went to help Mom take care of his things, I found journals representing many years lined up on the shelf above his desk. I wanted to claim them but was unable to take any of his books back on the plane. The following January I found the same type of blank book at Woolworth's and resolved to keep track of my own days—just as he had. (My books, too, now fill a whole shelf.) Much later I claimed Dad's journals and began to read, despite my fierce allergy to old paper. Mom had warned me repeatedly, "They really aren't much." She was right: These left-brain records were memory joggers to help him recall the details he would include in his weekly letter to all of us, scattered as we were across the country. The journals added little to the letters, which I had saved, with their trivia of place and work and an occasional personal note on the back.

Only last year I found more writing from his hand, pages I had saved but had forgotten even existed. They were letters he had written to me during my first two years at college, at his alma mater in Michigan. I read and reread the letters, most penned in his beautiful handwriting. A revised picture of my father began to emerge. He had loved me so much that he had penned letters to me between patients or while on trips. He had loved me enough to let me go when another man came into my life. Numbering one's days—which I seem to be doing more of these days—also means slogging through the hard work of getting the story right.

Dad would have loved Flat Iron Lake. Several years before his death, he convinced Mom to buy a piece of land from his brother, near his boyhood home, even though they owned a house in Texas and his job required traveling to hospitals in the Southwest. They drove their Airstream to Michigan occasionally and stayed as long as possible. He had a pole-barn built to house his tools and his vintage Oldsmobile Tornado, up on blocks. He loved to spent time there—reconnecting with the land. How I wish he could have shared our joy over this field and used his photographer's eye and ever-ready pen to preserve it, alongside Fritz

and me. I want to believe that in this setting he might have also responded to my longings and let me know him, little by little, in all his complexity.

January Thaw

Not only have our plans changed this month, but we're also in a thaw. We can't help but wonder about global warming when temps reached a record sixty degrees on January 8, and all the snow and ice leave us. The weather bug on my computer flashes warnings of fog, high winds, and flooding, but none of these threats slows us down. I can hardly remember the two feet of snow that complicated driving a week ago. In such nice weather, I'm even eager to return merchandise and find myself planning unnecessary trips to town.

We did use the dense fog as an excuse not to drive to church on Sunday morning. Truth was, we were supposed to be en route to Africa and just couldn't face all the questions from friends who thought we had gone. The fog did indeed hem us in, but it felt like a "gift day," one we hadn't expected to have and perhaps didn't deserve. A day without an agenda—no place to go and nothing that has to be done—is good for the soul now and then. And it reminds me that every day might feel more precious if I welcomed it as an unexpected gift. If I had only one day…one week… one year left to live, how would I spend it?

Three swans found some open water on Flat Iron and have returned. But today there are four. At first I thought it was a second pair—the yearling bringing home a "girl friend" for parental approval. Then I thought the new one might be a lost swan teaming up with this family because his own had disappeared. But I speculate, too, about other things—where were they when ice had covered Flat Iron Lake: Hunkered down on the ground or in some other open water? Nearby Wabasis Lake is much larger. I wonder whether it freezes completely. If they are migrating birds, why aren't they long gone?

I find myself doing the same thing with animal sightings that I always do when watching people: I observe them and their actions and then make up what I think is a plausible explanation for what I see. Whereas some observers are quick to make a judgment of behavior—as, for instance, either unbecoming or becoming—or to impute motives, I am just fascinated by possible background stories. Not only the scene unfolding in front of me, but their life story. With wild animals you don't tend to think of motives, plans, or feelings. But if I watch the swans long enough, the stories I imagine for them are very human. It's hard to think in any other way.

"I'm going on a walk—want to come along?" calls Fritz. I hesitate. It would mean leaving my book and the quietness of an afternoon not spoken for. "Well, Jake and I are leaving for the woods." "I'm coming—wait up!" I call back. "Only thirty seconds to make up my mind—give me a break!"

But I should have known. Not a Sunday afternoon goes by without him asking the same question about mid-afternoon. "Want to go cross-country skiing? Want to go bike riding? Want to…?" I tease him that this is a throwback to a time when his family always ate a big roast beef dinner, complete with abundant veggies and followed by a generous piece of pie a la mode. After an hour of semi-stupor from eating too much at midday, he'd feel guilty and decide to get some exercise. And even now, when we are more likely to make a quick sandwich after church, the impulse remains blazoned into his psyche.

I may hesitate, but I seldom say no. It's fun to walk with him across the fields or through the woods—in any kind of weather. New sights await us, and he's a walking resource for nature trivia.

Today, in mid-January, we trudge through several inches of heavy, wet snow past beaver territory. One of Mr. Beaver's accomplishments completely crosses the path. We speculate about how long the tree has been down. The pencil point of the break is still white in both directions, so the felling must have been recent. Another big one is not far away. Why does he pick such thick-trunked trees? Once down, they're impossible for him to move. He gnaws off smaller branches, but the major part is left behind. His castle of piled sticks mounds up not far away.

As though the beaver has set the agenda, today becomes a "tree-walk." In this mature forest, the trunks tend to be branchless until they are several stories high. Fritz estimates one to be over 100 feet tall, with foliage only on the top quarter. I almost lose my balance trying to gaze all the way to the top. When these trees are leafed out, many of their characteristics are hidden. I spy a large, hollow trunk still standing straight (although topless), about twenty feet tall. Its surface is pocked with elongated holes where the woodpecker has found his daily bug breakfast. In the early morning Jake and I perk up our ears at his rata-tat-tat. Other trees lean, as though they are about to topple. Another has fallen but never made it to the ground before getting caught in the crook of a neighboring tree. We see a single trunk that divides into three distinct trees partway up.

Fritz can identify trees by their bark; I'm limited to leaves, and that only in the fall when they begin to differentiate themselves. The beech tree hangs on to its tannish-gold leaves; even though they fade and become paper-thin, they alleviate some of the starkness of a forest in winter. The oak leaves hang on too, but curl as though used up. But all around their base and into the woods, acorns that have eluded the squirrels are planning to sprout for the next generation of oak.

The air is still today. Just a little wind can make even these gaunt trees sway and creak. After a windstorm we usually see a few old or weak trees felled. We leave them lie, knowing that even in death they will bring life to the forest creatures.

The only time we harvested wood from this plot was after a line storm that passed this way one night the first year we lived here. In the aftermath we found many vibrant trees snapped off like matchsticks as though by a monster hand. Maple, cherry, oak and ash lay on the forest floor. Our son-in-law moved the valuable wood with a forklift and stacked it in the nearby open field. Then we found a man with a portable saw mill to cut the fresh wood with its long, straight trunks into boards of various lengths. They're now stacked in the barn, curing and waiting for a carpenter to give them new life.

Before leaving the forest, we saw evidence of deer, both by their prints in the snow and by the worn tree bark they've used like sandpaper to smooth their antlers. Jake noses around what looks to be a brush pile that surely shelters some other hearty woodland creatures. There was a time when vines about two inches in diameter hung on many of the trees—perfect for kids and old men to swing on them like Geronimo. Fritz reluctantly cut down many of them when naturalists told him they were another type of invasive plant that could eventually choke the trees and

Cross-Country Skiing

impede light from reaching the ground. Some of those vines now serve another purpose—a housing project for forest rodents. Too bad the doorways are so small, or Jake would have made a Sunday afternoon visit. Instead, he just moves along with us, sometimes far ahead and sometimes far behind, as only his nose directs him.

The tree shadows lengthen as the sun begins to set behind us. Sunday afternoons are at their shortest in January, so we head home. We've come full circle, gather-ing winter sights and sounds and wondering about all the wildlife that Jake sniffs but we never get to see. One day soon, when the snow is deeper, we'll don our cross-country skis and glide the same route on another precious Sunday afternoon.

DELIGHT IN THE DAY

"This is the day the LORD has made; let us rejoice and be glad in it." (Psalm 118:24)

I love to begin the day watching the sunrise advance. If the first things I see through sleepy vision are many distinct clouds, I know it will be a good one. Just time for a shower before I sit with my morning tea and watch the slow-motion moving picture. In my theater there can be no artificial light, only natural illumination that seeps through the clouds and into my window.

It's not easy for me to sit still that long without reading or eating or jumping up to empty the dishwasher or just beginning the work of the day. But the sunrise holds me there to just sit and think—my mind is busy enough. The day past, with its sufficient worries, is prayed away and replaced with a fresh slate. God decorates the day, offering possibilities for good or ill, as I choose.

In her book Receiving the Day, *Dorothy Bass writes, "Across the centuries, in countless languages and cultures, Christians have adopted shared patterns for speaking out loud that this is the day that God has made, a day given to us only once, a day in which we are invited to live in boldness and creativity." Every day is the day made by God, not just Sundays, as I had somehow come to assume when the words of Psalm 118 set to music were the first I heard from the pulpit every Sabbath morning: "This is the day (echo), that the Lord has made (echo). We will rejoice (echo), and be glad in it (echo). This is the day...."*

Now I sing the antiphonal chorus any day of the week as the black and white picture of morning takes on color. Clouds make the most striking transformation, and the contrast from start to finish is as different as Kansas is from the colorful kingdom of Oz. They're gray on their undersides at first, but from the still hidden sun those clouds slowly absorb multicolor, until I no longer notice their darkness.
This is the day!

Dear God, My sunrise vigil encourages me. Your sun always rises, with or without me as witness, investing a new day with life and hope.
Amen.

Little Bluestem

Whether creation happened at one moment or over time (days or millions of years), one thing is clear: Each created thing has a built-in mechanism for preservation. Animals reproduce; plants propagate. All species bear a distinct set of genetic markers that contain the code or blueprint for the next of its kind.

What looks like death in winter contains the potential for life when the conditions of temperature, moisture and light are favorable. Gradually evidence appears: Baby bunnies are jumping from the underbrush, and shoots of crocuses and tulips are poking through last year's matted foliage. The potential of bulbs doesn't surprise us as much as the mustard seed or the little bluestem's feathery pods. But as spring turns to summer, bunnies turn into moms and dads, a shoot of bluestem becomes a widening clump, and birds perch on the branches of the mustard tree. We see that everything is going as planned.

We think the species we see will go on forever, but then we remember the bones of dinosaurs at the natural history museum. Rare animals, which were once plentiful, join the endangered species list while their eggs and sperm are banked in case of calamity. Elaborate seed banks have been created in certain parts of the world to protect seeds, with their ever-present life potential, in case some natural disaster wipes out certain crops.

Civilization continuously encroaches upon natural habitats. Our job as Earth-keepers is to preserve and restore wild places so they don't disappear. National parks, wilderness areas, nature trails and city green spaces need to be guarded too. Because our life span is relatively short, we must teach creation care to our children in the hope that they'll pass on their awareness to the next generation, who in turn will honor creation by preserving it.

Learn more:

a country year: living the questions
by Sue Hubbell (Random House, 1983)

Earth-Careful Way of Life
by Lionel Basney (Intervarsity Press, 1994)

This is my Father's world, and to my listening ears

All nature sings and round me rings

the music of the spheres.

This is my Father's world; I rest me in the thought

Of rock and trees, of skies and seas;

his hand the wonders wrought.

Snow Capped Prairie Coneflowers

Creating and Sustaining

How do words become emblazoned on one's soul? Set them to music and sing them at least once a week in school when you're young. The words will never leave you—or so I have come to believe. Six decades after repeatedly singing "This is my Father's World," I wake up before dawn with the words of this song on my mind—not just the triumphant lyric "all nature sings" that became the title of this book, but every word.

This is my Father's world, and to my listening ears
All nature sings and round me rings the music of the spheres.
This is my Father's world; I rest me in the thought
Of rock and trees, of skies and seas; his hand the wonders wrought.

This is my father's world: The birds their carols raise.
The morning light, the lily white, declare their Maker's praise.
This is my Father's world: He shines in all that's fair;
In the rustling grass I hear him pass, he speaks to me everywhere.

This is my Father's world, oh let me ne'er forget
that though the wrong seems oft so strong, God is the ruler yet.
This is my Father's world; why should my heart be sad?
The Lord is king, let the heavens ring. God reigns, let the earth be glad.

I pull the old hymnal from the library shelf to verify my recall. I can remember happily singing, in chorus with my classmates, these lyrics in praise of nature and of God, its Maker. I don't remember anyone in those youthful days dwelling on the wrong seeming "oft so strong." Perhaps we thought we would not be obliged to handle those realities in grade school. But on this particular early morning that wrong overwhelms me.

Part of the reason I woke up early was because of new concerns over the political situation in Kenya, East Africa. Fighting and bloodshed, burning and looting threaten my Father's world in a part that I love halfway around the globe. Friends are in danger, and there is nothing I can do about it. Wrong is strong. On days like these, God's rule and sovereignty over all created things seems tenuous. If you own this world, God, why don't you make it behave?

Isn't that the crux of the disparity between belief and unbelief? The question of "why" seems to be the litmus test of belief: For what possible reason could God have either allowed or caused this terrible thing to happen? Questions fill my mind. If you're real, God, and if you brought all of this into being, why can't we see your hand in control in this universe? Long ago we rejected the idea that you set this world into being and walked away from it, letting it run on its own.

How God chose to bring life into being will always be a mystery. He could have used a big bang, or he could have instantly formed living creatures as we know them today, or he could have used some other method. But God's decision to uphold or sustain everything he has made may be far more crucial than the act or acts of creation. Somehow, all things

> ## "I want to see the wonders of my God on display–in dynamic forms that live and move and have their being."

God made had to keep on going; living things are no more clock-like than the world itself. "He's got the whole world in his hands" is such a sweet picture, but life is neither a snapshot nor a freeze frame. Every second all living things move, change, grow or die.

The Creation Museum opened recently in Kentucky. While science and theology issues are very important to some, for me the more vital concern is not how God did things in the past but how he is working today. Perhaps there should be a Sustaining Museum. I want to see the wonders of my God on display—in dynamic forms that live and move and have their being. God knew that people of free will continuously ponder things they do not understand: hearts that beat, rivers that flow from unknown sources, an Earth that orbits the Sun and frogs that wake up on the first warm day, ready to sing.

Nature and human nature were both created by God. And while that belief does not answer the burning "why" questions that come when life seems unfair or violence erupts or tectonic plates move and cause tsunamis, it's eternally comforting to know that God's promise is still ringing from the heavens: "I will never leave you nor forsake you." (Joshua 1:5) God reigns—and I'm glad.

February, 2008

February stands for tradition. During the dreariest month of the winter, when the snow is crusty and dirty and spring only a mirage, I think back to the time I saw my fiance's hometown for the first time. Piles of plowed snow rose higher than cars or people at each intersection in Muskegon, Michigan. The snow-mountains were covered with soot. I almost got cold feet.

More than fifty years later, I have Muskegon to thank for saving February. Amidst its paper mills and foundries and harsh, lake-effect winters, a group of guys became friends—a friendship that has lasted for half a century. Every February, this group gathers for homecoming celebration at our alma mater, Calvin College, not entirely out of loyalty to the college but mostly on account of loyalty to each other. Seven couples keep the annual February date sacred, almost like a religious holy day. We travel to Mecca.

The Muskegon core has been an open circle, later incorporating roomates and inevitably the women who saved the guys from singleness. Even we foreigners from Pennsylvania or Colorado and from Borculo or Holland, Michigan, have inherited the group loyalty. But the Muskegon recounting of escapades, gradually revealed in unguarded moments, brings back the glory days of youth. Hanging out at West Lake, chipping in on a $22.50 1937 Ford from Mrs. Hewitt, releasing homing pigeons with leg-streamers at the biggest basketball rivalry of the year—are just a few of the threads that hold us together, year after year. Each of us, whether original members of the gang or not, latches on to the strands that grow thick as a rope with each passing year.

What kind of cord can hold people together this tightly? Tradition! As the fiddler once proclaimed. We have watched this tradition strengthen through shared experiences, trust and a curiosity about how each of our lives continues to unfold, in ever new and unexpected ways. Tradition could imply being stuck in the past—but not a chance with this group. Some things have stayed the same, but when we talk I'm nearly always amazed at how progressive and active our discussions become.

In the last few years we've eaten at the same restaurant, with tables facing each other in an open square for better conversation. After we eat our fill, we give the floor to one couple at a time so they can tell more about their lives—the good and the not-so-good. We've been together too long to deny that suffering is real and present in all our lives. We pass around pictures of our children or grandchildren but rarely go on about them unless they have a particular need.

Our shared love and loyalty grow taller each year just like the tallgrasses—even as our bodies shrink and crumble in small ways. Together we've weathered unusual and near-terminal assaults to some of our group—cancer, internal bleeding, heart attacks and an organ transplant. Together we've shared the pain of our children's divorce, infertility, depression, job loss and disability. But we've also shared triumphs.

Without talking about it much, we clearly also share many values. Each of us remains an active member of our church, all within the Reformed religious tradition. We all attended Christian schools, many of them fledgling, struggling to stay afloat while maintaining some level of quality. Most of our children followed our example or our money and attended the same college we did. Our former careers run the gambit. Believing as we Calvinists do that anything we have is ours in trust, we continue in retirement to give back to our communities, schools and churches through local and world-wide volunteering. No marriage has ended, no spouse has been lost, and after a rash of serious illnesses during mid-life, all of us are relatively healthy. We don't agree on everything—we are surely bi- or tri-partisan—but we are ready to cross the aisle, at least in discussions.

We are pre-Baby Boomers—all born before 1945 and all products of the "Greatest Generation"—the children of the children of the Depression. We inherited the thrift, as well as the generosity, of our parents. We laugh about some of our irrational quirks, like using a tea bag more than once and washing and reusing plastic bags. Although I would never try to check this, I doubt that any of us carries debt, even in the form of a credit card balance. We all vote, recycle, care for our parents, stay in close touch with our children, have regular physicals, and tithe from what we have.

As I walk the slushy driveway today, I'm reminded that the choice to honor our friendship is not unlike the decision to stay with a spouse through any adversity or to continue to attend church every Sunday. Our circumstances will change over time, but we have vowed to stay together "in sickness and in health, until death do us part." None of us can let the others down. But more than that, all of us feel that we're loved and know that this motley crew will be there for us, come what may.

We are a microcosm of one segment of our generation. Whether typical or not, we jealously hang on to our cult of friendship. And in the process, the Muskegon gang saves the dreary, lifeless dregs of winter, the month of February.

In Sickness and in Health

In 2007 I returned from our Africa trip very ill. It began on a stopover in London, and on the last horrible night Fritz and I wondered whether I could make it home. Our doctor son-in-law advised us to just get home. The transatlantic flight was a blur. During a series of weather delays, which included four hours stuck in a plane on the tarmac in Detroit, I coughed uncontrollably. The next morning an x-ray showed the culprit: pneumonia. With medication I slept for days, hardly able to raise a proverbial finger. Fritz waited on me, and I felt worthless. The doctor warned me that pushing myself in any physical way could trigger a far more serious relapse. I searched my library for a challenge, and there it was: *God Awaits You: 30 Days with a Great Spiritual Teacher* based on the Classic Spirituality of Meister Eckhart.

I found a fresh spiral notebook and enrolled in Eckhart's school. The small book contained a translation of this ancient mystic's words from Latin, in four segments per day: my day begins; a single sentence thought for the day; my day ends; and an evening prayer. Uncertain where this Bendictine would take me, I also found a text each day from Romans 12 that matched or contrasted with the words of Eckhart. And, as had been my custom for some time, I meditated on the words, prayed them and then wrote down what came to mind.

Journal Entry

On February 12, I read these words: "We have different gifts, according to the grace given us" (Romans 12:6a), and "Your works depend upon God for their authority and not upon yourself; you are merely the agent" (Eckhart). And then his prayer: "May all my actions point to God." My journal entry from that day:

> *Sunday was renewal day. Until this morning, I had not so much as put my toe out of the door to test the weather. After my husband left for church, I figured a week was long enough to be in bondage, so I bundled up with my heavy sweatshirt over my neck-to-toe bathrobe, a scarf around my neck and a ski hat. I was amazed that the temps seemed moderate and I was able to walk down the drive to the barn with Jake. But my fragile strength soon ebbed and I returned to sit back down at this, my 1st floor desk. Mental work was still easier than physical.*

> *Sick or well—gifts are dependent on God's grace. But once the gift is entrusted to an individual—God expects it to be used "in proportion to his faith." The agent must have faith that God placed such a gift in his/her hands for a purpose. Eckhart reminded me that all the actions of the person entrusted must point to God the*

giver *"of every good and perfect gift." I will never forget that God gave me back my life twenty-five years ago after a sudden illness. God proved he was not done with me then or now. "Can the dead praise you?" the Psalmist once said when pleading for his life. And so I pray with Meister Eckhart not only for life but also for the will to follow his words, "May all my actions point to God."*

I had no such insight back when I was "sick unto death" in 1979. After two months in a hospital bed suffering from internal bleeding, I returned to my home skinny as a rail and totally devoid of energy. Family life swirled around me while I sat. Day after day I sat, much as I am doing these days, until in my boredom I took up pen and paper. Even lifting the pen and keeping it moving was hard. But eventually I wrote, in an almost unrecognizable hand, a page a day. The pages piled up as I came back to life. Writing saved my life back then, and it can save this life again. And dear Meister Eckhart, who called me from a library shelf in a time of need, left me with that singular life-call: May all my actions point to God.

On a hoar-frosty morning, the switch-grass plants take on a regal air. The stalks are so graceful and unsubstantial, but with the added girth of moisture they expand and glisten. Each top resembles an artistic scepter. Looking

Switch Grass

through a stand of them almost takes my breath away. The browning foliage too, clumped around the stems, is equally delicate with long narrow leaves, curving at just the right point and accented with translucent water particles.

Switch-grass plants stand tall in the prairie even after they lose their color and dry up. The stalk that holds up the seeds, while skinnier than a toothpick, still often stands several feet high. Because the first snow fell so gently this year, none were broken or bent. If I were to try to pull up even one plant, I would find myself unable because the root structure below ground is as deep as the foliage above is tall.

I've heard that switch-grass has been targeted as our next potential source of bio-fuel. Because of those glorious roots, it can be harvested one year and grow just as tall the next. The idea of burning it sounds far-fetched, but so did the burning of corn a few years back. If only we could come up with a way to produce bio-fuel from switch grass without using fossil fuel. Here at Flat Iron Lake we've burned switch grass, along with the whole field, not for our benefit but for the enhancement of the plants themselves. Their ash seeps down into the earth and promotes the growth of the next generation.

We'll preserve our native switch-grass. Someday specimens of it, along with other native grasses, may be as rare as museum pieces, just like the open, undeveloped land they sit on. But on this February morning, switch-grass is just plain lovely.

Simplicity

Simplify, the gurus tell us—return to nature. Well, here we are in the middle of more nature than one could ever take in, but that doesn't make life simple. I can, for example, simplify my lifestyle but not what I take into my mind. The two simplicity robbers that won't leave me alone are true marks of modernism—the TV and the Internet. Both bring wonders never before imagined but also carry the problems of the world right into my quiet study: the deadly war in Iraq; the upcoming election and its hoopla, and troubling situations on the streets and in the villages of Kenya. For the first time in my life, my sleep is disturbed some nights because the problems of the world and the distress among my own circle of caring press upon me. In the middle of the night I find myself wide awake—not with wonder but with a vague, undefined fear.

As an antidote Fritz and I latch onto things of beauty wherever we find them. Yesterday we watched a pair of beavers or muskrats playing by the edge of the ice, which is again forming from the tail side of the lake. Usually the beaver's activity is barely visible; a large, v-shaped troubling of the water is a clear sign of his presence, but we rarely see more than the tip of his nose creating the wake. Our binoculars are always handy, but getting a good view has proven elusive. The beavers today were definitely up to something. Fritz dragged out his tripod and most powerful lens but still couldn't capture their activities. The next day these guys were back on the ice edge that by now had filled more of the open water.

Today my husband's camera captured the red ball of the sun coming up over the horizon. That light show unfolds quickly, but because of the beavers' antics, the camera was poised and ready to capture it. And so we have a few moments of peace and grand simplicity before hearing the insistent call of our devices to look beyond nature into the wider world. We have returned to nature but are still not free from life's complexity.

February, 2000—Walking

Making a vow and keeping it may not always be simply a matter of will. For example, take my vow of walking each day to get the mail. That presumes that there will be mail—supposedly neither rain nor snow nor sleet can prevent it from coming thorough. And indeed, I find that after eight years in this rural spot there hasn't been a day missed, except for mail holidays, like Martin Luther King Day and Veteran's Day, which I always forget until I realize that the top box is empty and only the newspaper slot is filled.

But on mail days, will there be anything in the mailbox? Sadly, if it weren't for my friends from Citibank offering yet another credit card three times a week, solicitation for charity, and waves of campaign rhetoric, each with its own pleas for funds—many days my mailbox would be empty. I love to find handwritten greetings from friends, but most of those have given way to e-mail missives. Each day I find a small stack of mail, but volume doesn't equal value—just more to recycle.

The vow also presupposes that each day I'll be able to get out of bed, stand on my feet, and move one foot in front of another. Walking is more "pedestrian" than running, which is the domain of an elite few whose feet and legs, lungs and heart can sustain such rigor. As much as I used to love running, a sport I took up for a few years in midlife, walking has been my mainstay pleasure. I cannot take this ability for granted, knowing so personally from my son, who can't use his legs, that each day on one's feet is a marvelous blessing.

My prayers have often included thanks for feet that "toe" neither in nor out and can be relied upon to carry me wherever I want to go. I've never had a broken leg or even a sprained ankle. But one day, early in our life at Flat Iron Lake, the little twinges I'd been feeling on those first steps out of bed turned to deep pain. Each step to the mailbox hurt; I couldn't ignore it.

The doctor showed me the x-rays and delivered the news: plantar fasciitis. The young doctor was surprised to know that I'd never worn spike heels or otherwise abused my feet. His prescription was foot exercises and special shoes. I'll never be as compliant a patient as my husband, but keeping my feet healthy felt like a matter of life and death. The shoes were not as bad as I had imagined—neither high-tops nor sensibly ugly old lady's shoes. The stiff wooden soles were in fashion with the younger crowd, and once I had adjusted to them they made me feel a little "hip." Until, that is, a fancy dinner came along or an occasion when a dress was best. But my husband couldn't understand my slavish compliance:

"For just one night couldn't you wear decent shoes?" No—my feet are too precious.

Over a number of months the pain lessened, but the doctor's order rang in my ears—you'll have to wear these shoes forever! It seems as though I already have. But good feet rank right up there with sharp eyesight and hearing for enjoyment of this prairie—perhaps a small price to pay for a daily walk down the driveway and an ongoing life on two feet.

I invested in some wide sports shoes with the stiffest sole possible, along with a pair of German-made sandals especially targeted toward the plantar problem, so I'm not altogether trapped in the clogs. I even found clog boots, but walking the uneven ground on the prairie still takes its toll on my feet. So, for a while, the smooth, paved driveway is the best place of pilgrimage for my feet and me.

UGLY CLOUDS

"Thick clouds veil him, so he does not see us as he goes about in the vaulted heavens." (Job 22:14)

Not all clouds are beautiful. Living in Michigan, close to water, and accustomed to cold, snowy winters, I know that dark days are part of the landscape. The view from my window remains colorless through clouds so thick that the light from the sun comes out gray. I worry about people who need light to avoid depression because there is no "partly" in the forecast today, modifying either "cloudy" or—how I wish—"sunny."

This Sunday morning my husband and I joined other worshippers in a brightly lit church and felt God's presence filling us to overflowing. But outside that clear and radiant place, I felt my spirit deflating like a balloon with a pinprick leak. Before long I could no longer revive the hope that had so recently satisfied me. I longed for last week's beautifully bulging snow clouds, and even for the heavy snow that covered the grime of the city. As we made our way home, even the country appeared cheerless. God seemed to have gone into hiding.

Perhaps it was on a dark day like this that Job felt abandoned by God. Although Job's friends reminded him that God could see all of his shortcomings, he was convinced that God saw nothing—including, and especially, his misery. He wondered whether God could see anything, much less judge him, through heaven's vaulted darkness. We, with Job, find it difficult to believe that "...the darkness and the light are both alike to thee." (Psalm 139:12 KJV)

Each of us handles gray days differently. My husband opted for a walk in the woods, which pleased the dog greatly. I declined for a change and curled up with a book, letting my mind find another place with weather more favorable than my own. When the sun couldn't push through the clouds, I imagined many people grabbing a warm quilt and escaping with a Sunday afternoon nap.

Now it's Monday. Today's ground fog has lifted, but still no sun has come to color the day. I no longer have the leisure to grouse about the weather; work has a way of pressing upon me its demands—rain or shine. But Sunday's rest during a thick-cloud day offered me a break in the action that sunny days seldom do. I remembered days past and saw them as they were, not always bright and beautiful, but full of goodness and full of grace. Even ugly clouds cannot stop God's everlasting light from streaming its warmth straight into my heart.

Dear God,
Gray days are not my favorite. But all days are your gift, even though clouds may shroud the sunlight. Help me see your light and life through winter's darkness, both outside my window and inside my heart.
Amen.

"Planned obsolescence" is a phrase once used to describe the intentional manufacture of goods that wouldn't last. While it may have been a viable business strategy that increased demand and profit, making goods with a deliberately limited life span leaves us with lots of junk. Outdated clothes, glasses, single-use containers, cars, appliances—need to go somewhere when we no longer want or need them. Modern packaging has made purchasing more convenient, but it has at the same time produced a mountain of waste.

Since the days of saving everything usable, including cooking grease for the "war effort," most of us have allowed someone else to worry about the second or third usage of cans, bottles and boxes. When our rural trash collector discontinued the biweekly recycle pickup because of low subscriptions, the rapid buildup in our garage waiting for a trip to the recycle center distressed us. Seeing the accumulation from just two people boggled our minds, especially when we mentally multiplied our pile by millions of consumers.

Some cities are making it more convenient to recycle, but many folks don't take the time to sort the recyclables, preferring to simply add them to the trash headed for the landfill. But once we become sensitized to the second-use principle, we find the habit almost impossible to shake. Those Cheerios™ boxes, plastic bags, and sour cream containers ("Dutch Tupperware") have to go somewhere.

Children of children of the Depression of the 1930's know this deep within their bones.

God alone made things out of nothing. But we can be "creators" too—repurposing discarded things into something useful or recycling things that would otherwise have been destined to become obsolete waste. When times are good we might ignore trash; when scarcity returns, though, frugality may too. And not for our profit only, but for the good of the whole Earth and all that dwell therein.

A recent headline announced that "Our economic pain is landfill's gain." The year 2009 marked a downturn in the economy, and in the same way that consumers reduced their gas consumption when the price topped $4 per gallon, so they are now buying less and tossing less. As one garbage collector put it, "The trash man is the first one to know about a recession because we see it first." That can't be all bad. At last report in 2007, Americans recycled 63.3 million tons of trash and composted 21.7 million tons—but we also burned 31.9 million tons and discarded 137.2 million tons into landfills. When the economy suffers, we can learn valuable lessons.

Learn more:
www.epa.gov/recyclecity/
Want to teach your children about recycling? Play these interactive games.

"…blessed are your eyes, for they see, and your ears, for they hear. Truly I tell you, many prophets and righteous people longed to see what you see, but did not see it, and to hear what you hear, but did not hear it.

(Matthew 13:16-17)

Finch

March madness hits us with horizontal rain on this morning's venture down the drive. I hoist the stadium umbrella, trying to ward off the rain, holding it sideways to shield myself from the stiff breeze and hoping it won't turn inside out. "At least it's not snow," some say, but today I'm not so sure. Early spring rains share none of the beauty of later rains; they chill you to the bone and chill your spirit with their gloom. It doesn't take long to realize that there's no romance in a morning like this, and we hurry inside so Jake won't get any more soaked and bring in that disgusting, wet-dog smell.

I think of all the field mice and voles whose winter dwellings are now leaking from the thaw. Before they finish mopping up the water, it may freeze again and leave a little skating rink in the living room. Neither mice nor men dare to declare that spring is just around the corner. We know better. We'd prefer a gradual easing from freezing, but erratic thaw and freeze is what we'll get. We dread but expect another mighty deep-freeze or a large dump of wet snow before this winter is out of here. Only the guy who plows our drive, who we pay by the push, prays for more snow.

If my driveway pilgrimage is like other spiritual quests, March resembles the "slough of despond." Like Christian in Pilgrim's Progress, I'm discouraged; I can't rise above the misery of the harsh weather and pervading deadness all around. Walking or just peering from my upstairs window at the flattened earth with its aging snow piles under sky of sullen grey, I share the lifeless aura of nature. "Rejoice in the day," I tell myself, but my longing for a renewed Earth overwhelms me. Earlier on in the season, deep in a Midwest winter, I have no such angst—things are supposed to be that way. But in pre-spring (as my Dad once said, "We're rational animals—but not very"), I let nature's gloom creep inside my psyche. I dare speculate that "This is my Father's World," with its cheery line "he shines in all that's fair," wasn't written in March in Michigan.

> "I dare speculate that 'This is my Father's World,' with its cheery line, 'he shines in all that's fair,' wasn't written in March in Michigan."

At Flat Iron, next to our drive near the house, we have a real slough (a deep bog), better known in these parts as a swale. Natural debris and living things in amazing biodiversity are trapped underneath the ice, which due to the heavy brush and trees that ward off fleeting glimpses of sun will take its time to thaw. Spring begins in this bog. But for now, while cold lingers, I can only imagine the sound of the peepers—those little frogs that pierce the air with their high-pitched sounds, announcing the end of winter. I know why they wake up singing. They too have been deadened, hibernating in a barely alive state, until the time is right. If they could reflect like humans, they might blame themselves for the sinful burden of despair. Aren't six decades of springs proof enough? Why can't I rise above this late-winter suffering? Ash Wednesday, as I well know, always leads to Easter. Again in the words of my favorite hymn, "Why should my heart be sad?" When Lent began this week, many excesses competed for my vows of abstinence, but now my greatest sin is not being able to give up grousing about the weather.

Easter falls in March (at this writing in 2008)—much too early for a full, vicarious appreciation of resurrection glory. Dark winter coats and shoes to match belie the finery of the most holy day on the Christian calendar. We need the color of daffodils, along with warm breezes and the music of tree frogs. For now, the promise waits. Creation groans, stirring right there under the ice of the swale, but I can't hear it. I catch only the sound of my own groaning: Will spring ever come? "Which of you," in Jesus' words, " if his son asks for bread, will give him a stone?" (Matthew 7:9) Or, if she asks for the squishy new life of spring, will God tease her with endless frozen earth? I want to wake up… singing.

Other Kinds of Madness

Heavy rain gives an eerie cover to the surface of the frozen lake. Yesterday the ice fishermen were out on Flat Iron all day. They believed the forecast (which some of us have begun to doubt) and savored their last day of sport before the thaw. It may take a month for the thick ice to melt, but when the surface is covered with water it looks unsafe. Early in the ice-fishing season, as well as at this time of year, we hate to see the die-hards out there trying to extend the season. Fritz and I fear that we might witness one of them falling through the ice and be forced to respond to a dangerous situation. From our vantage point, with almost the entire lake in view from our kitchen window, it would be hard to ignore.

Even if fisher-people do play it safe, there's something maddening about folks getting such pleasure out of a sport that most of us are too chicken to get cold over. One man often comes before dawn, sets up shop with no protection from wind or cold, and leaves as the sun sets. He sits alone. What goes through his mind hour after hour? Maybe he's getting away from a nagging wife to this quiet place. I don't understand his passion, but for his sake I'm sorry to see the beginning of the end of his seasonal getaway.

The freeze-and-thaw cycle of March creates madness on the roadways, too. A driver never knows whether the surface will be snow-covered and slippery or just deep in slush. One day puddles and the next "black" ice. And then one morning you see a big puddle ahead and too late you discover that it's a crater filled with murky water, just waiting to grab a tire and knock it out of alignment. You almost need a pothole scout—riding shotgun.

This year the road commission has overspent because of the hard winter's snow plow costs and has let it be known that there are no funds remaining to fix the inevitable potholes. The mayor of a city nearby was chauffeured on a "What are you going to do about this?" tour through the city streets. Mad Michigan motorists always come out of the woodwork—or shall I say the asphalt?—in March. We've witnessed something new out here in the country: sections of road just churned up and mixed with gravel that will harden—waiting for time and money to lay new pavement. Small signs give scant warning of this low-budget alternative: "Pavement Ends"!

March has become pivotal during the primary season for the 2008 national election. It's Super Tuesday, and I find myself drawn into the madness of politics because I have thrown in my lot with one candidate. I hope the majority of voters share my view in what some have disparagingly called "mania." I watch the news channels and check my Google News several times a day to keep up with the latest. But the news gets me worried, especially when campaign tac-

tics are thrown in to distort the picture. This is crazy—not only the competitive fray but also the reality that I can't stay above it. I wish I could just check in tomorrow and see what happened while I slept. My emotions rise and fall with the delegate count.

The only March Madness that I truly love is witnessed on the basketball court. There's order to this madness, though—the gradual process of elimination. Not all the teams that qualify to advance are expected to be competitive. But that's the fun of it: The dark horse, the underdog and the least-likely-to-succeed all have a chance. And that makes the whole process captivating. And these contests, unlike the presidential primaries, have rules we all know from the get-go. We may not like a referee's call or the other team's aggression or the home team's advantage, but we can't complain about the rules. After the field narrows from the sweet sixteen, the elite eight and the final four, there will be a champion. And if it's our team that becomes the NCAA champion, we'll carry that winning glow for years, like Fritz and I have for the Michigan State Spartans.

A few years ago we traveled to Tucson during March Madness. We might have preferred combining the trip with winter sports as we've done in years past, but our work took us to the sunny Southwest. After walking without jackets in already warm Southwest temps and sharing basketball evenings with our friends, we returned to Michigan late one night to find deep snow clogging our driveway. By the blue-white light of moon and stars, we slid off the drive and got completely stuck—and then had to trudge, without boots or warm jackets, past the quiet bog, through the white stuff to reach our house—with its heat turned down.

Nothing about winter looked beautiful that night, but by the next day the March sunshine sparkled off the new-fallen snow. The plowman breezed effortlessly down the drive, probably chuckling at our marooned car. We retrieved our car and suitcases and began to wonder: Is there time to do a little more cross-country skiing before this late-winter snow turns the paths to mud? That's March—lovely in spite of all its madness.

Nature Watch | *Ice Shelves*

I feel like a kid some mornings when I stomp on the ice shelves along the drive. The black pavement attracts heat from the sunshine, even before the temps rise above freezing and melt the nearest pile of snow. Overnight the melting snow turns to ice and leaves a suspended ledge sticking out about a half inch from the ground. The crack from one footfall is never enough—I stomp with my right foot down the drive to the barn and then all the way back. I'm glad only Jake is watching my folly. It's the crackle I love, along with the feeling of power that destroys without hurting anyone. Perhaps the separated ice chunks will turn liquid today and run down the slope of the drive—one more subtraction from the residue of winter. Tomorrow more ledges will appear from

heat trapped underneath the snow, melting another layer underneath the ice. My foot would like nothing more than to smash more ice ledges, until neither snow nor ice can withstand the warmth of spring.

Journal Entry

March, 2007—I don't know which of us is more excited. The killdeer are back! After last year's delight in watching a pair nest on the rocky path and produce young killdeer right in view of our bathroom window, we welcome their return. Fritz once again (see account in May from a previous year) installs his camera on a tripod with two legs in the bathtub and begins to record their mating and nesting. Such unusual little birds, with their dark neckbands and long, skinny legs. Every morning we check from the window and occasionally peek into the nest. Eventually there are the requisite four eggs, pointed ends meeting precisely in the middle. The pair takes turns keeping them warm.

They like us: Our home is their home. But it's early March, so much earlier than last year, when we watched nesting and birth after Fritz's surgery in May. I read that they can have two broods some years if the conditions are favorable. Last year the wildflowers and grasses offered the newborns ample cover, but this time of year the fields are still flat.

Early April, 2007—For a few days we smiled, watching the nervous male trying to play decoy with his cackle and wounded-bird routine. One of the pair is always on the nest. But then, after one night's hard frost, they are gone. I race outdoors, not wanting to believe that the show is over. There is the rock nest, no more than a slight disruption of stones, completely empty. A foot away I find a fragment of shell.

Maybe our home isn't so hospitable after all. Other critters live here too, some of whom relish fresh eggs. Perhaps they froze first and then were found. We may have a preference for killdeer over groundhog or fox, but the plans of life are out of our hands. As I walk down the driveway past the field that was recently burned, I hear the killdeer call. They're hard to see in this camouflage, but if I look closely I spy a little, black-striped head bobbing in the distance. Perhaps they will try a less public place this time, but it's not in their nature to hide. I'll keep watching—from a distance— wishing them success.

Sightings | *Wood Ducks*

Wood duck boxes dot the western shoreline of Flat Iron. Large birdhouses on poles sit a few feet off shore, where the spring melt begins as the days warm. Our neighbor Bruce usually waits for a sunny day in March before checking out the boxes. By the residue he can tell by how many eggs were laid, hatched or remain intact whether last year was a good one for ducks, who prefer to nest in a dry, safe box rather than on the ground. We understand their reasoning when we watch the annual trek of ancient snapping turtles up the hill to lay their eggs.

Bruce calls with his annual report. Expressions from Fritz, like "You've got to be kidding!" or "No fooling!" let me know he's talking to our nature-loving neighbor, who eagerly shares unusual natural phenomena. Bruce had opened the hatch and reached into the dark wood-duck house nearest his home, only to be met by a live animal snapping back and then leaping out, nearly brushing Bruce's check. "I nearly lost it," he reported with a laugh. He wasn't laughing when the raccoon escaped, though. And now we all scratch our heads. How did such a large animal force its way into such close quarters? Did he enter as a baby, feed on unhatched duck eggs, and then just hibernate for the rest of the winter? Was he roused from slumber by Bruce's footsteps and ready to jump as soon as the hatch was opened? I can't help but add my human speculation: Did his family miss him? Come looking when he didn't show up for dinner? And all these months later, did they rejoice over the return of their prodigal son?

Another Parable

Parables fascinate me; they are the ultimate extended metaphor. To explain why he used parables, Jesus taught his disciples by referencing the prophecy of Isaiah:

> "For this people's heart has become calloused;
>   they hardly hear with their ears,
>   and they have closed their eyes.
> Otherwise they might see with their eyes,
>   hear with their ears,
>   understand with their hearts
> and turn, and I would heal them." (Matthew 13:15)

People of Jesus' day had closed their senses to understanding. They looked away from his bodily presence and closed their ears to his illustrated stories that taught profound truth. But Jesus turned to his followers—and, I believe, to all of us who also turn away:

> "…blessed are your eyes because they see, and your ears because they hear. For I tell you the truth, many prophets and righteous men longed to see what you see but did not see it, and to hear what you hear but did not hear it." (Matthew 13:16–17)

I've heard many sermons on the parable of the sower. Not many of us are "sowers" who spread their seed by the broadcast method. In fact, my spell-check always marks the word—it would like sewer better. What if each person's vocation or avocation was substituted for the noun "sower" when reading this parable? Thus, the following paraphrase of Matthew 13:3–8: "A writer went out to write. And as she wrote, some words blew around on hard places, trying to anchor, and then just blew away. Some words went out and grew quickly but because there was no depth to them, they wilted in the heat and died. Some words couldn't quite distinguish themselves from all those other words out there, so the downbeat ones didn't make room for the more hopeful ones. Finally, some words dropped on open hearts, hearts that grew richer and fuller because of them."

With a little contextualization, the sower-or-sewer-or-writer parable takes on new meaning. Each of us has our own medium for understanding and furthering the kingdom. Despite the obstacles that invariably stand in the way, we keep trying: more stitches, more seeds in different soil, more and better words. Jesus used literary devices, like parables and poetry, to help people understand the challenges of a life with him.

Many prophets and disciples had the same yearning we do: to see and hear God speak to us. My time on the prairie has become just that: a time to look and listen for "glimpses of truth" that I long to grasp and then to pass them along to others—perhaps those of closed eyes and inattentive ears.

A Parable without a heavenly meaning…(the story of our own fight with tares)

I can't help thinking about an actual sower out here on the prairie. Even though I've never seen a farmer planting seeds by the broadcast method, I remember those pictures from my children's story Bible—of a man in a loincloth with a sling-sack hanging around his neck, tossing seed in all directions. I've never experimented with planting seeds in varying types of soil. But even the amateur grower of house plants or the occasional planter of a flat of annuals has experienced the hard dirt resulting from forgetting to water those plants that looked so promising in the store. Or the disappointing results when we think we don't have to work the soil or remove the rocks before planting. But the situation mentioned by Jesus in another parable I know all too well, now that we've tried to restore a prairie. That's the scenario where seeds have to compete with tares (i.e., thorns or weeds; see Matthew 13:25–40 in the KJV for that intriguing old word).

Even though this parable, like all others, has a deeper meaning, I'm opting today to use it literally. Nothing frustrates a farmer more than a piece of land that refuses to accept the seeds he throws onto—or plants into—it. Just such a piece of land lies close to our house on the north side of the circle drive. Its south-side cousins have been blooming for years after their initial planting. The north side was too narrow for the DNR's long-armed planter, so Fritz decided to seed it himself, sower-style, as he had earlier done along both sides of the long driveway.

After the fall seeding and the ensuing winter, once the earth had given up its snow and the sun had warmed it for many days, we waited for the first sign of growth. To our credit, we were patient. Since grasses and wildflowers require years to take hold, and small plants are hard to distinguish from small weeds—our waiting only produced a longer time period for the invasive plants (i.e., tares) to take root. Finally, the field of weeds became an embarrassment, and Fritz arranged for a planter with a small rig to come in and churn up the earth before planting a mixture of grasses and flowers. Another long wait, after which our hope drained. All the while the other fields were flourishing and had already sustained their first "controlled burns."

When people came to see the fields of flowers, we steered them away from the "poor relations" toward the colorful side. Fritz found another guy to kill the invasives and plant yet again, this time forgetting the flowers and concentrating on one type of grass, little bluestem. We watched something come up and hoped against hope that it was the prize we were looking for. While we waited, though, the thorns once again pushed down more roots and were ready to go to seed. Fritz mowed them down and called the guy back. The two plotted and planned. There must be some way to rid the field of those choking sprouts.

No other portion of our land has been disturbed as much as this one. The ground was rocky and often packed like a path, while not ten yards away butterfly weed and little bluestem were waving from a ridge near the vegetable garden. We knew they had to grow. In the fall the parcel was ripped up again and a layer of Roundup™ applied. Talk about an eyesore! After all the vegetation had died back, new seeds were drilled into the earth. Winter came, then spring. We tried not to look very often, for fear our eagerness would jinx the field yet again. Finally, little mounded clumps of spiny green pushed up. Would bigger, heartier weeds be ready to defend their territory and squelch the little bluestem? Would the soil turn hard in the summer heat and choke them from underneath the ground?

The trouble with the parable, as we read it, is that we tend to think the farmer knew the fate of his field right away. Not until the second winter did we know for sure the fate of this planting. The first snow fell lightly around the grasses. Yes, even around the grasses on the north side of the circle, between the house and the swale—and little bluestem began poking up everywhere. Not long ago Nate, the tall college student who helps us out, repeatedly plunged his shovel into the hard ground between the thriving, good plants to remove the invasive weeds. He created mounds of tares that dried in the sun. I'm pleased to make the announcement: After eight long years, the sower is finally winning—at least twofold for now…and—do we even dare to hope?—maybe later more folds.

When the real parable calls the planter of the weeds the devil, I believe it. So, just what is the lesson in this modern parable?

Leaping

More than a foot of snow fell overnight. We're tired of the white stuff that has been so abundant this winter. I pull on my boots and follow Jake out the door. While I trudge through yet another accumulation of wet snow, he leaps. His long black torso curves with every jump. As his front paws return to the ground, his hind feet continue to fly; when they come down, his front side is into the next leap. He delights in every bound, like a hurdler overcoming one more barrier. From a distance he looks like a squiggly black line on the horizon. Deer have the same graceful curve as Jake, but black on white is more dramatic. Even if I were as excited as he is about this new batch of snow, my body would have no way of showing it. Our own play in the snow, whether on sled or skis or skates, is so tame in comparison. The closest thing to that kind of fun is when our grandkids set up ski jumps and challenge each other to fly off them.

When Jake was only a pup, he went crazy in the snow. He'd make circles around us and now and then dip his nose into the fine powder, as though hearing or smelling something below. We started chanting "Run around, run around!" and making exaggerated circles with our arms. In the same way he's a sucker for chasing a ball or stick long past the point of exhaustion; he'll go in circles until I get tired or cold. He has no limit. He's older now, midlife in dog years, but "Run around!" still elicits the same response—a frenzied run in large circles around me, amid flying snow. I can almost see

him grinning like a kid who "can't get enough of that wonderful stuff." I smile too, even though I've certainly had enough of this stuff that no longer seems so wonderful.

Recently I listened to a man talking about the importance of play among us hard-working humans. "If you forget what play is," he invited, "just watch a Labrador retriever. They never outlive their readiness for play." Thanks, Jake, for reminding me that a little leaping won't hurt me, either, as long as it's only in mind and spirit.

The Lion and the Lamb

"The wolf will live with the lamb,
 the leopard will lie down with the goat,
 the calf and the lion and the yearling together; and a little
 child will lead them." (Isaiah 11:6)

The lioness of March roams restlessly stalking her prey
The field, the sky, the barren woods abound
with dreary sameness
Colorless but for discolored snow.
Listen as she roars, then croons then whimpers in pursuit of spring.

The wobbly lamb lingers in warmth of fold
Mother Earth will not let him play alone
For storms or sudden frost or prowling pride
March on, ready to pounce.

We watch and pray—
Enfold him 'til sun's warmth overcomes cold,
'Til birdsong opens each day
'Til he meets that mellowed beast who cradles him as her own
and a babe beckons: "Follow the leader!"

C. Rottman, 2009

The part of the woods we visit most often is the gently rolling terrain on the smoothest parts of which a path has been mowed. But a short distance away, on either side of this relatively flat area, are two large ravines that are underwater or damp year around due to heavy tree cover. The runoff from one of those ponds feeds the little stream that eventually crosses the main road.

Within the woods are a couple of frog ponds—places where water collects and aquatic life abounds. Toward summer's end the water is bright green with algae. Our biologist friends call the woods an eco-preserve—a forest left in its natural state to maintain and enrich its resident native plants and animals.

The driveway to our house bends around a large swale, which is about the size of a narrow football field. Because of its heavy brush perimeter, we've never explored to its center, where fallen trees float and many creatures make their homes. It's a natural collector of surface water from the ground that rises along its banks. The bees live in hives nearby and use the swale as their watering hole. Several duck families also nest there—a safer place than the lake with its hungry snapping turtles. Frogs and toads are often heard calling from the swale but seldom seen.

The loop of the driveway by the house circles a garden. Instead of the raised mound we had envisioned, a wildflower grower advised us to make a water garden, a depression that is fed by the rain runoff from the house. Certain wildflowers love water and germinate even when they're submerged. Narrow, wet ditches and troublesome low spots in yards can become water gardens and with almost no maintenance add great beauty to a dull landscape.

Learn more:
See "Growing Native" by Neil Diboll in Birds and Blooms, April/May 2009, for a list of wildflowers and the types of soil in which they thrive.

Weather conditions must be perfect for a burn: dry but not too dry,

a gentle breeze without gusts, and enough of last year's thatch for fuel…

The fire leaped dramatically, higher than a three-story building,

and then smoldered into dense smoke.

Controlled Prairie Burn

ALL NATURE SINGS: A SPIRITUAL JOURNEY OF PLACE

April alive: I see it everywhere. On the fool's day, the weather seemed like some practical joke. The day began deliciously warm—prepared, it seemed, to drain the puddles and the land that had filled from the downpours of the last days of March. Then the wind came up and blew in a wave of cold so bone-chilling I could hardly brace myself against it on my way down the road. The sky hung gray, dampening my enthusiasm for new life, but once back inside I heard some commotion outside my bedroom window. The fat robin we had spotted only days before was scurrying around with nervous jerks. I thought she was looking and listening for worms in the moist earth, until I saw several other robins in a haphazard dance— a mating ritual, I presume. "First comes love, then comes marriage, then comes robin with…nest building materials." About this time each year, one frustrated suitor usually attacks his own reflection in our bedroom window, waking us with a loud pecking noise, dulling his beak but scoring no points with the opposite sex. He persists—unrequited love is hard to let go.

> *Never yet was a springtime when buds forgot to bloom.*
>
> *Margaret Sanger*

Already the finches are sprouting their yellow feathers—dapple green isn't going to attract the ladies. Oh, the calls all those birds make this time of year. It's downright noisy early in the morning, as male and female try to attract each other from the treetops. The redwing blackbirds call with a clear, pure sound. I hear the scratchy caw of the sandhill crane long before I see their long, flexible necks waving above last year's grasses. Yesterday one sandhill called and another answered from somewhere across the tail of the lake. I imagine she had found a place to call home and wanted him to join her. Many birds fill the air with sound but move too fast for me to identify. In April I always wish I knew more about birds and their habits. But this much I know: They have survived the winter and have come out singing!

At night, despite the fierce cold, Fritz joined our neighbor to witness the spring ritual of the beaver. "You've got to be kidding," he exclaimed over the phone, and I knew the caller had to be Bruce. Just last week I pointed out to a friend the beaver mound on the shallow

part of the lake, still landlocked by ice and white with snow. But as the ice began to recede from the lake's edge, I knew it wouldn't be long before the big guys would emerge from their hothouse and get to work. Because of heavy rain, the water level had risen high enough to cover our dock. Beaver prefer the level high as they rush to cut and drag trees along the entire lakeshore to the water's outlet near Bruce's house. We dock owners, in company with the nesting waterfowl, think it should recede naturally, but the beaver do their darndest to keep the water in their lake. It's good that Bruce is young and ambitious because he pulls the logs away from the outlet, knowing full well that the beaver will build another dam overnight. Both man and beast think they can win this tug-of-war, and both have the work ethic to prove it. It usually ends in a draw as the lake finds its natural level.

One day I saw a beaver up close—my first real sight of this creature that is usually submerged in the lake, with only the tip of his nose pointing the direction of his travels. Just before crossing the road at the end of our drive, I noticed something furry off to one side. The dark brown body lay unmoving, but I was leery anyway. It had none of the color variation of a skunk or raccoon, so I stepped a little closer. That's when I saw the flat tail, a little narrower but longer than a ping-pong paddle, and the long, webbed feet—belonging to a beaver, quite dead. I gave a little gasp as I moved away, crossing the road to get the paper. But there on the pavement were two large swaths of fresh blood. The beaver hadn't died of natural causes but had gotten in the way of a fast-moving car. Our drive is about half a block from the spot where Fritz observed the dam by the neighbor's homestead—the location of the beaver's last stand. Perhaps this beaver, which I imagine must have been young on account of his size, became frustrated by the hard work upstream and decided to check out the fast-moving stream flowing from the outlet.

I thought of the baby beaver all the way home—he had come out of hiding only days earlier, and now his life was over. Will others come to look for him? How do animals take care of their own? The next day Fritz brought his camera, and we looked once more: The long, sharp teeth that were powerful enough to saw through wood like a power tool; the huge, amphibious feet that look almost human except for the skin between three toes; and that funny, hairless tail that can announce to members of the tribe when trouble lurks nearby.

Fritz buried him so he wouldn't decompose above ground and attract other scavengers. It's hard enough for me to view death but even harder to smell decaying flesh and witness the remains after one beast has feasted on the innards of another.

Why am I shocked at death? It's as expected as life, but like any end it is difficult to accept. I know about the food chain, natural selection, even survival of the fittest within species, but I still hate to view death—especially in April when new life dominates the landscape. Just like my sadness when the last flower of summer was inadvertently mowed down last fall, I grieve the lost young beaver.

SIGHTINGS | *Wood Ducks*

Fritz and I seem to be on a perpetual nature watch in spring—each of us alerting the other to strange or beautiful things we see from a distance or up close as we're digging or planting.

4/23—From his desk window Fritz watched a purple martin perched nervously on the blue birdhouse. The iridescent black bird seems to have claimed this as his abode as the intended occupant watches from a distance. Monitoring the scene closely through binoculars, Fritz realized that the perpetual motion was the bird arching his beak down and pulling downy feathers from his own breast. Then he'd hover around the small hole and stuff the plucked feathers inside. Take and give—stealing another bird's home as his own but giving of himself to create a soft place for his mate to lay her eggs.

• • •

"You're going to be so mad at Jake if I tell you what he did today," were his words as I came home from town just in time for supper. Okay, tell me and we'll see if you are right, I thought. I never like it when someone thinks they know how I'll react even before I hear the news. It can't be that awful, I think as I ready all my "it's not so bad" feelings. But then the news comes: Jake has disturbed the robin's nest in the little white pine tree next to the garden walk. The pale blue eggs fell to the ground. Whether they were cracked on impact or by Jake's heavy paw or sharp teeth, I'll never know. But this I do know: These eggs will never crack open naturally, bursting with new life; a generation will be interrupted; and Jake deserves my wrath and a bellyache.

• • •

On a damp morning in spring old and young worms push out of their earth homes to sun themselves. As though stretching after a long sleep, they pull themselves to full length on the driveway and just lie there. No coiling, or wiggling, as they are known to do when a fisherperson tries to use them for bait. Movement of the worms is imperceptible; they look like motionless pick-up sticks scattered from a pile. I make my way between the multitudes, trying not to squash any. Jake thinks they look good enough to eat but changes his mind when he smells them up close. Anyway, he prefers critters that give chase—not these sluggish beasts.

If I watch long enough, I see slight movement in a straight line as the body retracts a little and then expands a few centimeters forward.

I must get to work, but if I had the time to watch for hours, I would see that even by this poky method they make tracks. When the sun lights the pavement just so, trails of secretion shine. At some point the moisture evaporates and the worms reluctantly maneuver into their moist earth homes. When I return to look for them, the hoards of earthworms have gone underground as though I were a predator. Dryness and hungry fish are their only enemies. Underground they live lives I cannot watch, until the next dewy morning or a warm summer rain allows them to make a beeline to the puddles and briefly enjoy the light of day.

April, 2002
Living by Fire

The Fed Ex driver rarely stops to chat when dropping a box on our doorstep. After a quick punch of the doorbell, she motors back down the long drive before I get to the door from my upstairs study. Our house sits in the middle of a vast field so far off the main road that no driver on the clock wants to take time for a signature. But this early April day she waits on the porch until I open the door with a question; "What happened to your meadow?" As we looked out over the charred field, I admit, "We burned it."

"But why?"

This year's controlled-burn was our first since taking over the acreage in rural Michigan six years ago, following my husband's dream of restoring a prairie. A week ago, on either side of the quarter-mile driveway there lay the remnants of last year's native grasses and wildflowers, arched to the ground from the heavy snow of winter. In the distance, a mature deciduous wood bounds the western side of the property, and the small Flat Iron Lake marks the eastern boundary.

Weather conditions must be perfect for a burn: dry but not too dry, a gentle breeze without gusts, and enough of last year's thatch for fuel. Earlier, we informed the neighbors by letter of the coming burn but couldn't specify the time. When the burners arrived one early evening, I wanted to send them away. The crew looked like those on a newscast fighting forest fires, and like the others, they must first start the fires in order to stop them. They began by torching a perimeter band and then quickly extinguishing it as a firebreak. Moving into the wind, they turned and set ablaze the next wider band. The fire leaped dramatically, higher than a three-story building, and then smoldered into dense smoke.

Suddenly the wind shifted, intensified, and carried flaming straw over the break toward our neighbor's house on the edge of the field. Another neighbor across the lake saw the flames reflecting in the picture window and offered help in rescuing their belongings from the burning house.

The pyrotechnics attracted fire-loving boys of all ages. One teenager reported for duty as a junior firefighter. The professionals had it under control.

Later that night, after the high drama of fire had ended, cars filed back out of the driveway. Only smoky mist and an acrid smell remained. Both seeped through our closed doors and windows or rode in on our clothing.

None of the frightful beauty of the fire greeted me and Jake on our early morning tour—only black, runted stalks of weed as far as we could see. In the weeks that followed, I averted my eyes from that awful, singed earth on the lakeside of the driveway, trying to imagine its promised renaissance.

Hope waned. I thought we had made a terrible mistake. Until one morning, when the rising sun helped me spy just a hint of green poking through the stubble. The next day more color. After three weeks green covered the land.

I thought of the delivery truck driver, and her question brought me full circle: Why? To encourage the plants that were once native to this part of the world, one must follow the wisdom of our first Americans and burn them to the ground. Native plants have deep roots that fires can't harm; invasive plants grow shallow, and flame robs them of growth.

Summer will come soon enough. The Fed Ex driver hopes for more packages to deliver—because now, new clumps of black-eyed Susans, coreopsis and persimmon-colored butterfly weed show themselves each day. During the warm months, many more native flowers and grasses will take their turn showing off. And as the days get shorter and the sun hides more often, along will come several varieties of goldenrod and New England asters—a splashy finale.

Although winter and fire laid the grasses and wildflowers low, they did not die: By fire, they live.

Little Bluestem

The migratory birds are back. Their sound and sight sometimes startle me as I walk through the fields. Three brilliant swans pass overhead, making only a slight wooshing noise but impressing me with their size and grace. Two are a pair, and the third looks to be a yearling.

Two years ago, when Flat Iron Lake was lined with spring algae, this pair or some look-alikes hatched one baby swan. We watched, secretly happy that it was only one, unlike the geese who hatch hordes each spring, all of whom want to call our little lake home.

The cygnet must have watched his parents fill up on the fresh greens and followed suit, not knowing that his system couldn't yet digest the fibrous plants. For days we watched the family floating and diving on the lake. Then there were only two. Later on we learned that our neighbors on the other side of the lake had noticed the baby swan listing on its side, unable to swim with its head up. They made a dramatic rescue of the little bird, but even a bird vet couldn't undo the damage of so much lead in the belly.

Now when the three white birds passed by, I am heartened by last spring's success. The replacement baby, I imagine.

> "Do they lament over their lost young? Do their hearts, like mine, grieve over lost life?"

The following Sunday it was finally warm enough to walk the woods. With Jake dancing alongside, Fritz and I surveyed the trees, brambles and fallen branches along the circle path. Not long ago little clumps of snow were still visible, but today's groundcover takes on the variegated brown of partially decomposed leaves, dry enough that our footsteps make a mild crunching sound.

Suddenly, a white patch on the other side of a heap of branches catches my eye. I hurry over to investigate. On the ground in a space a little longer than a shoebox lay some fluffy feathers, along with a few stiff and sturdy ones, about six inches long. Not a trace of the body. It could be none other than the young swan. Some predator must have devoured all but the fledgling's glorious white coat. I try not to imagine the grizzly feast. A fox? A hawk? A coyote? Does it really matter? The child is gone.

Again I think about this waterfowl's parents. Do they lament over their lost young? Do their hearts, like mine, grieve over lost life? Observing them, I find it difficult not to project human emotions on the birds whose story I'd love to discover.

Today I watch one majestic swan searching for food on the lake, close enough to serve as sentry over his mate on this year's nest. We don't dare to explore the shoreline for their home, knowing how fierce and strong a male can be when protecting eggs in the nest. This lake and these woods have not been kind to this swan pair—but still they come back. They have experienced life and death here—but it's spring, and the hope of new life never dies.

Dani and Morgan, my four-year-old granddaughters, arrive in separate vans amid a flurry of hugs and greetings. They want to be together; I want to come along. I tell the rest of today's Sunday dinner crew to grab a cold drink, fill up on the sharp cheddar and flatbread and set the tables for sixteen. "If you are hungry, go ahead and get the mashed potatoes ready." We're going to the woods to look for signs of spring, taking the golf cart because their legs are short and the woods are a long way off.

As I lift each little girl onto the golf cart, my tear-drop-shaped necklace dangles in front of me. "Pretty," says Morgan, "That's your pretty!" Dani chimes in, "Pretty!" Then they look at each other, startled, as if to say, "That's my pretty." The pendant was my husband's gift to mark our transition from work in Cleveland to a new life in rural Michigan, which also marked a passage of life that enfolded these two girls. Each time I leaned over to change a diaper or to play with one of them on the floor, the jewelry hung between us—sparkling within reach of a little hand grasping for the world. Long before either could form words—"Pretty," I'd say, "That's my pretty." I couldn't have known that each girl would see the pendant as her very own claim on me.

I wrap my arm around the girls at my side, reassuring them that I love them both. We pass the barn and head along the path beside a stand of trees that line Flat Iron Lake,

hurrying through a muddy low spot so as not to get stuck. Up the big hill at the cart's slow pace toward the wide path through the woods that Grandpa Fritz has recently cleared of fallen branches. "Keep your eyes open wide and your gas buggy ready to ride," the preschool teacher in me sings, "And nearly every evening there's a pretty kitten sittin' by your side." The words make no sense but sing us into the woods.
"I love you a bushel and a peck, a bushel and a peck and a hug around the neck. A hug around the neck and a barrel and a heap, a barrel and a heap and I'm talking in my sleep—about you, about you…" They both know this one—I've sung it to them since they were babies.

Only these two, of our eight grandchildren, have I known continuously since birth because of our move near them in this country place. Morgan's birth was a minor miracle—thanks to reproductive technology that allowed our son Doug to father a child as a spinal-cord-injured person. And Dani arrived while I was helping her mom manage during three-year-old Tori's bladder surgery. Suddenly daughter Sue went into early labor, while her husband was away taking his plastic surgery exams. I cuddled Dani before her daddy did.

The woods invite us with a slight rustling in the underbrush. We imagine a mother deer and her spindle-legged Bambi moving quickly out of sight. Birds of a feather call back and forth, while peeper and bullfrogs create a high-low chorus from the bog. Now we walk along the path on brown leaves recently freed from winter snow. They've lost fall's startling color but still rustle underfoot.

Jack-in-the-Pulpit

I point out the tall green stalks of skunk cabbage. "That doesn't look like a skunk!" one observes. "But if you pull it up or break a stem—it sure smells like one!" They hold their noses in mock disgust until they spy the trillium and Jack-in-the-pulpit they learned about last year. The leaves resemble each other so we move closer, getting near the ground to see the red-veined cap over the little stalk someone thought looked like a preacher. Now they spot a whole stand of three-petaled trillium, and I remind them that these rare flowers will cry if they have to leave their mothers. Dani spots some smaller flowers under the big ones—the last of this year's spring beauties.

Now the path is soft with sand-like dirt, and Morgan stumbles over a rise that looks like a miniature speed bump. It smunches under foot. Looking more closely, we see a slight cracking where the dirt log was pushed up too high and couldn't hold together. "Moles," I say, and Dani volunteers that her daddy doesn't like moles. "Neither does Grandpa—they built castles all over his lawn during the winter—and nearly ruined his mower blade the first time he cut the grass." We wonder how they live down there covered with dirt.

Beyond some brambles I see the white spot in the distance. From their vantage point, the girls won't notice the shoebox-shaped pile of white feathers if I don't take them there. I don't want them to see the remains of a yearling swan that brought tears to my eyes when I discovered it last Sunday. There's a cruel, dark side to nature—far from the animated circle of life they know from *The Lion King*. Soon enough they'll know things that aren't pretty.

Thwack! The mosquitoes have just caught our scent and want our blood. They usher us back to the cart and we rumble off—leaving them in our wake. Dani's curls and Morgan's thin blond wisps blow in the breeze we create. "Over the river and through the woods to Grandmother's house we go…." We sing our farewell to the smells and sounds of this virgin wood.

The aroma of roast beef and garlic potatoes greets us— the girls ahead of me, hand in hand. "Where have you been?" call the hungry family members. "Oh, the places we've been!" we echo Dr. Seuss. "Let us tell you. Bless the food, Grandpa, and we'll begin."

Spring's Transformation

Now it's the end of the month, and I know that contrary to my fears on that chilly fool's day, the month has been entirely different from March. In fact, it has been an absolute joy, with a string of warm and hopeful days that made me feel as alive as the nature all around me. I want to clean neglected closets, dig in the dirt and tromp in the woods each day so as not to miss any of the emerging flowers and squeaking frogs. But the calendar gets fuller this time of the year, and I discover that dates in the city suddenly seem inconvenient and unwelcome. Even the work at my desk gets done faster, with the lure of the outside beckoning me. In spring this place is all I need. This year April was not the "cruelest month," as T.S. Eliot once reflected in *Wasteland:*

> APRIL is the cruelest month, breeding
> Lilacs out of the dead land, mixing
> Memory and desire, stirring
> Dull roots with spring rain.

But his sentiment rings true: Memory of former blooms creates within me the desire to sluff off the dullness of hibernation in celebration of a whole new growing season, in order to match the world around me.

Fritz, the farmer, also comes to life. His built-in almanac of "right times" to do certain tasks tells him that he is behind—so much to do and so late. He digs the last of the carrots buried last fall, and we eat them gratefully. "I could use a little help," he says to no one in particular, even though I'm the only one within earshot. I remind him that the garden is his hobby, not mine, but that I'll do my traditional part of harvesting, cooking and preserving. But I also know that I'll give in when the time is right and begin going after those pesky weeds that rob plants of growth and the neat, leafy rows of their symmetrical beauty. And I begin thinking about where we could find a farmhand to fill in for me with this guy who could use a little help.

Early Buttercrunch Lettuce

Some wildfires begin, not by arson or careless campers, but quite naturally due to lightning. But no matter the cause, the reach and devastation of the fire may well be fueled by contributing environmental factors: destruction of natural foliage around new homes, dry conditions because of climate change and overuse of water.

Native Americans observed the aftermath of burning in the prairies and realized that following the burn there was revived growth of nuts, berries and seeds. They could protect their villages from uncontrolled fire by the intentional burning of the perimeter. Travel too, they noted, was easier over terrain that had been burned.

With the settler came the desire to clear land for farming and plow the soil. Turning soil by the shovelful was backbreaking tedium, so the steel plow opened unimagined opportunities.

The plow also opened the earth, offering fertile ground, not only to intended seeds but also to random inhabitants. Weeds and invasive plants thrived side-by-side with corn and wheat. Herbicides were developed to kill stray plants and fertilizers to nurture the farmer's choice produce. Even road building opened the earth and inadvertently allowed many weeds to flourish. Even road building opened the earth and inadvertently allowed many weeds to flourish.

Controlled burning is a good way to discourage the growth of invasive plants, while encouraging native species. Native grasses have deeper root structures that can lie dormant for years but spring to life if conditions are favorable. Fire reduces all the dried foliage to black ash that is natural fertilizer and also soaks up sunrays, pre-warming the earth in the early spring.

Large plots of land require the expertise and equipment of professional burners, who can safely start and contain a fire. Fields should not be burned in their entirety, but rotated so that the ground animals and insects have temporary refuge. After about three weeks the blackened earth turns green with new growth. A burned area will show a three-to-fourfold increase in growth during the next several years. When the biomass doesn't allow enough light to reach the plants, it's time for another burn. Fire gives a short but spectacular light show. Thanks to fire, prairie grasses, dotted with wildflowers, offer a long, slowly unfolding summer of color and beauty.

Learn more: http://www.tallgrass.org/fire.html

The delicate columbine leads the way—

ours a maroon over-petal with a yellow underside.

I love their springiness but can't help comparing them to the native

columbine in Colorado that grow abundantly on high mountain meadows.

Columbine

ALL NATURE SINGS: A SPIRITUAL JOURNEY OF PLACE

May belongs to my mother. I've heard people say that it's wise to remember a loved one, not on the day of her death but the date of her birth. I do celebrate her long life on December 11 but don't shy away from marking May as her month, the one in which she died at age ninety-two. Birth and death form the bookends of a life.

Memories of Casey, my mom, are bound to the land here at Flat Iron Lake. Of all our years together, most separated by distance, the three years she lived near us shine vividly. Maybe because they were her last; maybe because we finally reunited as mother and daughter. We were both at turning points in life when we discovered each other as dependable friends.

My sister Mary lives in town close to the retirement center, so she was able to provide Mom with steady companionship and assistance. I watched them come together too, also out of need and a deep desire to make the most of these years. Earlier Mary, my sister Sue and I had convinced Mom to move from Colorado to Michigan when her eyesight diminished, preventing her from driving. At age eighty-nine she decided to move, with all the confidence of a college freshman leaving home for the first time.

Learning to see nature once again is not merely an aesthetic opportunity. It is a moral and spiritual duty, a debt we owe to nature's Maker.

Lionel Basney

I wouldn't say Mom took her new home, Raybrook, by storm, but let's say she stood out among her peers as self-assured, outgoing and compassionate, even in this totally new environment. Most of all, she wanted to stay busy—so she volunteered and read and played bingo and cards and visited the sick. Raybrook was like the college dorm she had never known. And a coed dorm at that! We'd tease her when she mentioned men with whom she had formed friendships.

Her little calendar marked the dates to look forward to. She became a member of our church, so almost every Sunday she came to Flat Iron with us after the service. Her presence still glows in this place. I fussed over meals for her, complete with fresh veggies from our garden and some kind of homemade dessert. She never failed to compare our menu with the "stuff they try to feed me" at Raybrook. Assigned seats, standard menus, rules both written and understood dominated her life but couldn't clip her wings. She spoke up when things didn't suit her. Friends from church joined us around the table for Sunday dinner and found her tales fascinating. She expressed pity for her age-mates who had spent their entire lives in one place and with the same people. Her own cosmopolitan history was rich and varied, and she loved to share it.

In good weather Mom and I took rides on the golf cart into the woods and down by the lake; walking would have been out of the question. Just the two of us moving at a great-grandmother's pace into lovely spaces. She, like me, loved the colors and scents of the woods, even though she knew very few names or understood much of how trees and forest flowers grew. The trees canopied over us, but the sun still found its way in shafts through the dense leaves. Her questions were like those of a child—ever curious, always open to learning something new. The simple pleasures of togetherness.

Sunday afternoons were the highlight of her week. After our feast, now seated in the recliner, she religiously completed the Jumble puzzle in the paper and then "rested her eyes"—never admitting to real sleep even though her snores could be heard throughout the house. "Read anything good lately?" she asked often. It was hard to find

books without sex or course language and with a happy ending. If successful, I'd send her off with a book from my library, as well as a care-package of food.

Mom never wanted to miss a holiday with our family, even though the noise of eighteen people often bothered her. I suspect she turned down her hearing aid when the clamor of children got too great, especially at the Christmas party. She wanted nothing for herself but often remarked that "kids these days" get too much. Several years later, when simplicity reigned at our gathering, one daughter remarked that "Grandma would have loved this."

Today I finished the book *Circling My Mother* by Mary Gordon. One chapter was devoted to the perfume, Arpege™, that her mother wore, the scent of which always brought her to mind. Gordon's memories were multilayered, alluring like perfume is to many people. But to Mom and me fragrances have had the opposite effect—revulsion. I inherited her allergy/aversion to artificial scents, as well as to some heavily-laden spring flowers, like lilies. My memories of my mother are less subtle and more basic than Gordon's.

I never considered Casey a complex personality, like my father. She was unpretentious and straightforward—even plain, but comfortable with that simplicity. Her letters, which sustained me over the years by their regularity and sunshine, contained facts, not feelings. Life to her was quantifiable, just like the numbers she had mastered as an accountant. Adjectives and certainly superlatives were not in her vocabulary. She loved to punctuate her letters with a bit of homespun philosophy: "Do your best and leave the rest!"

One day when I was helping change her calendar date book to a new year, she reminded me to reattach the list of all the books she had read. If pressed, she could tell me about any book on the long list, but mostly she kept those recollections to herself. She read her Bible too but didn't want to talk about it. It was what it was, and she wouldn't let its mysteries confuse her faith.

Her main theological stumbling block had to do with suffering—especially for the old who were ready to die but instead suffered on. She once commented that this was the first question she would ask God in heaven. I can just picture the scene as she gives the Almighty a piece of her mind. The suffering of saints offended her sense of justice.

Mom, who never wanted to "put anyone out," once suggested that if she were cremated when she died, we, the family, could gather to remember her when it was convenient. Practical to the end, she maintained that this would be easier on her children living all over the country. My reaction was swift: When you're gone we will grieve, not when it's convenient. She talked no more of cremation— just asking that we keep the funeral arrangements simple and that her body be placed in a plain oak box.

For all Mom's concern about how and when death would come, hers was a peaceful walk through the valley of death. We knew she was bleeding internally, but she refused invasive tests to discover the source. Always in control, she decided to end transfusions when they could no longer keep pace with the loss, and she accepted hospice. On Mother's Day 2005, Mary and I brought Sunday dinner to her retirement center, inviting as many of the family as could come to join us around the table. Grandma Casey sat regally, despite her slightly matted white hair and darkened eyes. She ate roast beef and mashed potatoes and squash with the family she loved—and then prepared to die. We suspect that this was her last supper—that from this point on she refused to eat so that death would come swiftly. "Come Lord Jesus, come quickly," she whispered one day. And come he did—five days after Mother's Day—to take her home.

Soon after Mom died on May 14, 2005, I gathered my writings about her—all of which she had read—into a small booklet that I titled *My Tribute to Casey*. Until now I had never written a postscript or an epilog to those stories of Mom and me. Grief had to work its way naturally. She hoped none of us would mourn her too much, wanting us to just go on with our lives. I do go on, not immobilized by the absence of her wit and unfaltering love but still trying to understand her precious life, as well as her peaceful death. All of us have our memories, but mine include sharing the wonder of nature on golf cart rides over the acreage by Flat Iron Lake. "Being with" was her idea of greatness. I cherish her greatness in my life.

May, 2005
Kill—dee...dee...dee!

With the coming of spring...Distant, piercing cries of killdeer penetrate the wind. They are one of the signals I've been waiting for. The sharp, plaintive calls seem to arrive in advance of the birds themselves, gladdening cries that can fill a landscape. They come with the first crystal-melting breaths of March or early April, announcing that spring, too, is on the wing.

from *Swampwalker's Journal* by David M. Carroll

I watched in disbelief the first time killdeer nested next to my driveway. There on the rough, rocky ground, in plain view, sat this distinctive bird with its double white-banded neck and long beak. One killdeer stood tall on skinny legs, while the mate made occasional forays from the nest into the prairie grass and wildflower fields nearby. Often I examined the little hollow of a nest, expecting to find some fluff lining so common with other birds. Nothing but gray, sharp rocks. By all signs, this pair was not serious about starting a family.

One morning, however, as my black lab, Jake, and I rounded the driveway, we heard the piercing "Kill-dee-dee" and watched one bird swoop and cry as though wounded. We took the bait and followed him away from the nest, where Ms. Killdeer sat, unperturbed. During a rare moment when neither bird sat on the nest, I discovered four rather large, mottled eggs, almost invisible among the stones. They were neatly arranged with the pointy ends toward the center. Now I felt I needed to protect the little nest from Jake's sniffing nose or other inadvertent wheels or shoes. But my wise, nature-loving husband had no pity: "If they lay their eggs within a foot of the driveway, there's little you can do to save them." I should have known that the birds had their own protection. Each time I passed I saw the same, unmoved eggs. Then one day they were gone.

After that first encounter with the peculiar killdeer, I was disappointed when the pair didn't return the next year. I wanted to learn more, and this year I had my chance. Not only did the pair pick a spot on our rough, stone-pebble walkway between the house and the perennial garden, but they were also in full view of our bathroom window. And more importantly, we had a break in our usual busy schedule because my husband, Fritz, was recuperating from major surgery. The unfolding life of a new little killdeer family brought just the gentle diversion we needed. Early on, I happened to see the male making several indentions in the path, by prancing around in circles and pushing dirt and small stones backward with his feet. Of the three hollows, he and his mate just happened to pick the one that provided our best vantage point for looking

on. On one of his first slow walks outside down the stone path, Fritz spied the four eggs when he nearly stepped on them. Now he was quick to put up some markers, in his own attempt to "save" them.

Many mornings I'd casually walk by the nest and check on the progress of the eggs. Even with the markers showing me the spot, I could barely decipher them at first. The dog paid no attention to the apparently scentless eggs, but that didn't stop the killdeer from putting up a fuss and enacting that dramatic, broken-wing bird show. On days when the male spotted us on our early morning walk, he'd try to pull us off course by swooping and cackling down the path. Once he led me with his diversionary tactics over one-eighth of a mile from his nest, as I walked down our long drive in quest of the Saturday morning paper.

As spring progressed into hot June days, the eggs were rarely alone. Taking turns, the parents protected their unborn from torrential rain, high winds and harsh sun. The day I spotted a big old snapping turtle making his way up the path, looking for some "soft" gravel in which to lay her eggs, I panicked, unsure whether she'd also like some tasty bird eggs for breakfast. I grabbed the rake and urged the angry turtle past the little nest.

My husband set up his camera with two legs of the tripod in the bathtub, which borders the window. Periodically, I'd watch with the binoculars and call him when there was action on the nest. The adult birds took flight if we approached, so the window provided good cover. As in

We took our places behind the window to continue watching the show. One of the parents sat on the brood, feathers puffed out and rising slightly every few seconds, like a bellows, drying out the downy little bodies. I felt like I was in a birthing room. Later on one little guy stood up beside its mother, while another struggled to make it up the rise on wobbly legs. Fritz snapped a quick succession of shots with the digital camera from inside the bathroom window, with the blooming prairie as backdrop. Suddenly I realized something I should have known all along—that our show was nearly over. This home was only temporary. Within an hour, all six had disappeared into the underbrush.

The next morning I felt as though my whole family had gone off to college on the same day. I couldn't imagine what their lives would be like now. Jake romped around the field, while I wandered aimlessly near the vegetable garden on the other side of the house, missing my routine morning nest check. Suddenly the adult killdeer were swooping and squawking, and there was our birddog trotting toward me with a prize—a baby killdeer held softly in his mouth! "Leave it!" I cried. He obediently released the tiny thing, which stood, shook, and scurried back under cover.

How do parents control four unbounded chicks on a vast prairie? I couldn't watch because they moved away from the garden hunting ground, with its larvae, beetles and worms, for relative safety from enemies like us. At first I occasionally saw or heard the parents along the drive, probably watching for other predators. When they disappeared,

years past, we nearly gave up the vigil, as the birds became a usual part of the landscape. I wanted the awkward camera out of the bathroom—until a chance glance changed everything.

Both parents hovered near the nest. The one covering the eggs alternately sat and rose. I thought I spied movement underneath her when she stood. Could the little ones be hatching? Fritz hurried outside and carefully approached the nest, to the alarm and noisy cries of the adults. He quickly snapped a shot of the four fluffy little bodies snuggled close together with only their brown backs exposed. He retreated as the killdeer scolded.

I read up on their habits: The chicks are precocial, which means that they can move around and feed themselves shortly after birth. It takes twenty-four to twenty-eight days of gestation before they hatch, fully feathered and ready to forage for food. The parents watch them continuously and send out a sharp signal to freeze if a predator is near. The obedient chicks move again only after the "all clear" is sounded. After twenty-four days of brooding, flying lessons begin. Two weeks later they graduate into the sky.

I nearly put them out of mind, so sure was I of not seeing the family again. But last evening as Fritz and I walked down the drive, we spotted some swooping birds and heard the familiar "Kill-dee-dee-dee," overhead. Exactly one month and one day after they had left the nest, all six of them took flight, dive-bombing and calling, as if to say "goodbye."

Our time together was much too short; this family had gladdened our hearts for a season. We can't attract the killdeer with food or color—they'll come again only if our rocky paths suit their fancy. But next spring I'll listen for that plaintive cry in the night wind, and hopefully watch the male prepare another nest and court a wife to produce a new brood. And if our prairie is chosen, I'll take all the time necessary to witness another miracle of birth.

(C. Rottman, published July, 2007 in *Whisper in the Woods*, Michigan Nature Journal)

Nature Watch | *May Inventory*

On the last day of May, I made a survey of sorts: field entirely green, slightly shorter foliage on the burned side, flower growth thick and full but not yet blooming. Wild mustard and purple phlox offer such gorgeous color it's hard to hate them. I pull them about five yards back from the drive but know I can't eradicate them all. We call for help from a college student, but understandably final exams hold more urgency for him. I'm convinced that the invasive plants will outlive us in this place. As one type fades, new enemies appear. I watch the purple vetch thrusting its vines with their parallel leaves between the daisies and coneflowers but am powerless to stop them. They're as attractive as the native plants, but they are bossy, wanting to take over. Queen Anne's lace, as we poetically call the wild carrot, is still small but ready to establish its invasive beauty later on in the summer.

We've seen our first lupine—a pink one in the rain garden and a deep purple specimen along the drive, at first almost hidden among the phlox. The groundcover of wild strawberries and potentella is full and blooming—white and yellow, respectively. Jake's nose will let me know when the tiny wild berries are ready to eat.

Two days ago, mama snapping turtle laid her eggs in a soft but bare spot next to the upper drive. I get as close as I dare to get a look without disturbing or—worse—getting snapped by those ancient and powerful jaws or

Queen Ann's Lace (Invasive)

Purple Vetch (Invasive)

Iron Weed (Non-Invasive)

Rosinweed (Non-Invasive)

scratched by those claws that have recently moved what seems like tons of dirt to make a bed. I can't figure out the ancient ritual. A few days from now another animal will uncover the eggs, usually in the dark of night, and devour them, leaving nothing but the shells. If these animals are determined to reproduce, I'd think there would be a safer place to lay eggs, at least one they could defend against predators.

The rain garden has come alive since a good, soaking rain in mid-May. We worried endlessly about the dry conditions but now have an abundance of blooms and buds. The delicate columbine leads the way—ours a maroon over-petal with a yellow underside. I love their springiness but can't help comparing them to the native columbine in Colorado that grow abundantly on high mountain meadows. Next come the tall, stiff-stalked golden ragwort with their teeny, daisy-like blooms. On account of their numbers, they add a splash of color, standing sentry-like while other plants are building strength.

Near the house a droopy lavender horn with a white snapdragon-like tube bears an exotic name: hairy beardtongue. Next to it, a little, white, five-part oblong-petaled flower turns out to be a blackberry bramble. White bouncingbet is really an invasive but too pretty to go after. Farther down the drive, emerging from really poor or rocky soil, I see the hoary alyssum with one light bunch of white blooms on the end of each long stalk, looking as though they've been gathered like a bouquet at the base

and then wave on flexible stalks to the side. They are early—hearty and determined to stay around all summer.

I always see the beauty before the blight. One day Fritz discovered stalks of the invasive type of goldenrod overtaking one side of the water garden. He showed me how to tell the good from the bad, which at this stage is only by the way the leaves attach to the stem. Soon I'm on my knees for hours, sorting and pulling while he goes after the quack grass with Roundup™. This is tricky, as he must dip a double-gloved hand (latex near his skin and cotton outside) into the mixture and then wet each grass stalk from the base to the top. After about a week it will die back, destroying the roots. A visitor to the prairie once asked, "How much time does it take to maintain the wildflowers and grasses?" We've never made that calculation but assured him that it gets easier every year. At least, we assure each other later, the pleasure and the pain balance out as spring turns to glorious summer.

Marsh Marigolds

THE GREAT PRETENDERS

"Therefore, as it is written:'Let him who boasts boast in the Lord.'"(1 Corinthians 1:31)

Clouds would be little more than partly transparent masses if it weren't for the light of the sun and the moon and their placement in the contrasting background of sky. The bigger and thicker the clouds, the more they hide the very orbs that make them so lovely. Then, when they are saturated with moisture, their color turns dark and foreboding. Either in the gray days of winter here in the Midwest or at any time storm clouds are ready to break, they can be bearers of bad news: The sun is not going to shine on the parade, or the picnic, or the pony ride. Sometimes when clouds block the sun we let it ruin our day.

But the opposite can also be true. Clouds can "bask in reflected glory" and thrill us with sunsets and dramatic skies. I went to college in Michigan, which has far fewer sunny days than my Colorado home—especially in the winter. We students from faraway places that were known for beauty, like Southern California and Washington State and Colorado, just loved all the attention we got from being identified with those places. We milked it. We basked in it. Over forty years later, I heard feedback of what students from more common places felt: We were just like clouds—not much all by ourselves—but ready to puff up a bit. Every time I mention that Denver is my hometown, I wonder whether I'm still basking. Or claiming that I'm a Christian, for that matter, without showing it.

Reflection isn't enough. Wherever we come from or whoever our parents are, the prestige of our profession says little about who we are. Folks are still going to search for what we're made of, and most of the information will come from watching us in action. Reflection may get a moment of attention, but unless we're colorful workers for Christ, we'll be among the greatest pretenders.

Dear God, It's so easy to bask in your reflected glory. When the dark days come, may we show love instead of lolling like mindless clouds, waiting for the sun to shine through us. Amen.

Wild Geranium

In the euphoria of new life that comes with spring, it's hard to think of death. The death of animals and birds, flowers and grasses, as well as of the people we love. "Dust to dust…" are often the last words spoken over a casket as it is lowered into the earth. But living things never really disappear—their matter takes on a new form. The woods often contain many "dead" and rotting trees. They become food for other living things, such as insects, which in turn feed animals and birds.

Without death there would be no new life. That amazing flower of the field couldn't withstand the wind and cold or rebel against its innate growth cycle and just go on producing forever-plastic blooms—but its seeds do survive. Animals, birds and humans also pass along their blueprint from generation to generation. Physical remains eventually revert to dust, but their essence lives on in following generations. Before the discovery of DNA, people saw likenesses to generations past but didn't understand how those copies of multiple characteristics survived death.

Watching a field that has been burned come back to life is an amazing display of death-to-life. In less than an hour, fire can reduce an entire field of stubble to ash, black and ugly by any standards. But the ash attracts the sun, warming the ground, and rain drives the ash deeper, fertilizing the dormant seeds. The stronger plants, those that are native to this part of the world, thrive, while the opportunistic plants cannot compete. All those seed pods that dropped or flew around on wings at the end of the growing season, as well as those that came in packets for the garden, are essentially dead—until the conditions of soil, water and light bring them back to life. They carry the blueprint of their kind.

In spring's celebration of life we also celebrate death—the gateway to new life.

Learn more:

Forest ecology and more: www.wisegeek.com
http://environment.nationalgeographic.com

Before fully embracing my life here on the prairie, the mountains seemed the only place to find God. Today I know that God sings to me every day through nature and grace right here. The ecological implications are clear—wherever God speaks is sacred ground.

Honey Bee on Butterfly Weed

June is one of the busiest growth months of the year, but it's also the slowest for caretakers. While nature works overtime, putting out one bloom after another in assembly-line fashion, our role diminishes. Natural automation, I think. Even the invasive plants that we fought so hard in May are crowded out now by native species and dying back, although their seeds will go on to live another year. Now that the gardens are planted, our main job is to water and weed—and, of course, watch. We now pick the asparagus sparingly so that the plants will stay healthy and go to seed. The rhubarb puts out giant seedpods, while the stems get woody. Soon I'll be picking a few strawberries every morning, if I can get there before the birds, who are already circling overhead for that first hint of red. The same is true for the mixed greens that are just ready for salads. So far I haven't seen evidence of bunnies, but you never know when one will sneak in when Mr. McGregor's gate is left open.

June is bustin' out all over.
All over the meadow and the hill!

Buds're bustin' outa bushes
and the rompin' river pushes

Ev'ry little wheel that wheels beside the mill!

from Carousel

This morning I found three new flowers bursting out: the cow parsnip, coreopsis, and ox-eye daisy. The milkweed plants with their upward-reaching, broad, scoop-like leaves seem to grow several inches a day long before putting out the baseball-sized head of tiny purple blooms that precedes their trademark pointy pods. The redwing black bird does not challenge me on the drive anymore, so I assume the babies are hatched and both parents are busy bringing home the insect-bacon. The first brood of geese, whose goslings seem to have matured overnight, have come and gone. I think neighbor Bruce has had something to do with their decision to find another lake with other docks to mess up.

The robins didn't choose the spaces underneath our deck for their nest this year, so I haven't witnessed their continual delivery of worms. We have, however, watched several robins on the hunt. They seem to have a sonar sense; sometimes they bop about a foot off the ground before honing in on a worm just beneath the surface. It's hard to believe that worms make any noise; maybe they emit a smell. Fritz is irritated because the big redwing blackbirds are dominating the birdfeeders and not letting the smaller, prettier birds enjoy the seeds. I'm reminded that we like some creatures better than others. Plants too. This morning I had to admit that the space the cow parsnip foliage takes in the rain garden is far more than its unspectacular bloom should claim. And as much as I love the waving coreopsis, they multiply quickly, last all summer, and seek all the attention.

June will be a slow month in the garden. Waiting instead of working reminds us that "but God who gives the increase." (1 Corinthians 3:7b, NKJV) Fritz, the resident master gardener, worries, as is his habit, over his plants and the moisture and unwanted bugs, but there is little more he can do to affect their outcome. I'm glad he has a fishing trip planned for this weekend—you can always see change after a few days away. Of course he'll leave me with a list of danger signs to watch for as well as remedies while he's away. I'll take my turn at getting away as soon as he comes back.

A Pattern

"Let there be spaces in our togetherness, so the wind of heaven can dance between us" (Kahil Gibran, paraphrased).

At the time, we thought this wedding vow of young friends was odd. No "'til death do us part" or anything comparable. But the longer we've been together, the wiser it seems. Parting at death will inevitably be painful for one of us, but occasional parting now offers each of us something the other cannot offer—spaces in our togetherness.

As often as I remind Fritz that I've registered for a writing workshop, when the time comes he grouses, "You're going to be gone a whole week?" I know my husband wishes me well and always gets along fine on his own, but having to think about meals is a chore for him. In contrast, life is not half so complicated when he leaves me; I can make a favorite pasta dish and eat it for the whole week.

Slow June is a good time for me to leave the prairie and Fritz in order to hone my skills—to go back to school. Summer school, you'd have to call it; perhaps remedial work, like many students take to catch up to grade level. I sometimes quip that "I've gone to school all my life" and will have to admit that some of it was a review of what I had learned earlier. There were large gaps in my educational pursuits; due to circumstances, I couldn't complete the process in one straight shot.

When I look back, I know I should have been an English major. But I lacked confidence and experience in literature. If only someone had responded when I made those juvenile attempts at writing prose, "Good start—now make it even better," instead of slapping red marks across the page and making disparaging remarks about my spelling and, I assumed, my ideas. Without the advent of the computer, I might have stalled out completely. Decades later, as I was working on my doctoral dissertation and took time off to master that new-fangled contraption before finishing the manuscript, I couldn't yet understand the computer's saving graces. I viewed its use as a practical means to an end. How wrong I was—it was a means to a beginning. Spell Check eventually alleviated my major stumbling block.

> "This turning point in my life would lead to a writing business, as well as the ability to pursue a creative writing passion."

Much too late, it dawned on me that I wanted to write—in fact, I wanted to spend the rest of my life doing it. "If wishes were horse, then beggars would ride" was another of my mom's wisdom sayings. Wanting was a good first step, but I'd need horses—to pull me along. Books about writing went only so far. That's when I realized that summer school might be the answer. Back then I needed to reclaim the summer, which had fallen into other uses, much like reclaiming this prairie.

In the late 1980s my project director job offered me three weeks of vacation per year. The time was easily used up by our annual trek to the Colorado Mountains, which had become a family tradition. I also needed time off for attending board meetings (an elected position) in another state three times a year. At first I took those days off without pay, but one day my boss informed me that since it was not local volunteerism, I would have to use vacation days. I was determined to work for the life I valued, so I made the bold suggestion that my contract be changed to allow me to work only four days per week. That way I could continue to work five days and bank an extra day every week.

Grant writing was my specialty. I really never toyed with the idea of doing that work independently of a job until I took a one-day seminar titled "How to become a Paid Independent Consultant." The leader mapped the route so convincingly that I couldn't get "independent" out of my mind. A few weeks later, my boss announced that my colleagues, although they were aware of my reduction of pay, were jealous that I could take days off at will, while they were tied to a schedule. Decision time: Give all my time and energy to this job or leave for a new life.

I chose the latter—thereby reclaiming all of my time, including my summers. This turning point in my life would lead to a writing business, as well as to the ability to pursue a creative writing passion. Both in left-brained grant writing and in a freer, right-brain expression, restoration would happen. The first would help feed my body with bread on the table, and the second would feed my soul.

The Summer Writer's Workshop at the University of Iowa was my choice. Each class offered a tremendous focus on one aspect of writing, and the experience took place far away from home, with a whole new cast of characters and freedom from usual demands. Total immersion—a great way to learn something new. For twelve years, as soon as the Iowa catalog came out, I'd choose the teacher and the course and pour my energies into preparation. Much as Fritz does when he anticipates his annual hunting trip to North Dakota, I lay out my tools, polish the required writing, and count the days. The first day of class always begins on a Sunday, so I have to start out early, miss church, and drive the seven hours to Iowa City. The first turn out of the driveway already seems liberating; hours alone on the road are a good launch pad for summer school.

I had no reason to consider another venue for summer school until the year Fritz had surgery on the thumb of his right hand. Neither of us knew how debilitating this would be. Over the years we've enjoyed a pretty strict division of labor where the garden is concerned—he plans and plants, while I pick and cook. But under the circumstances, I planted the little seeds in the peat-pots with tweezers and, when they were big enough, transferred them to bigger pots. A few weeks later, on my hands and knees, I nestled them into the ground. Just when his hand was on the mend, we got the news that a lump on his knee needed to be surgically removed. Post-op, he could neither bend nor stoop, so weeding also became my domain. Of course, he needed a chauffeur too—we were almost joined at the hip. I couldn't leave him.

I found two writing workshops at a local college and signed up. I didn't expect the magic of Iowa but couldn't help making negative comparisons. So much for total immersion—I was still tethered to home. My own distraction may have colored the experience, but neither the leader nor the group of twelve really bonded. Providentially, however, I sat next to a man who mentioned during introductions that he had a book ready for release, about making a spiritual pilgrimage on the Camino de Santiago. We exchanged ideas at every break and in the end agreed to exchange books. His book planted a seedling that June, and this book is one of its fruits.

Planting the Seeds of a Pilgrimage

Arthur Paul Boers walked the 500 miles of the Camino de Santiago, an experience he recorded in *The Way Is Made by Walking* (Formatio, InterVarsity Press, 2007). I put his book on a pile for later reading until I came upon an article he had written (Christian Century, 12/25/07)— a review of other books about spiritual pilgrimages. Another writer, Daniel Taylor, with whom I've had some contact, authored one of the books. Perhaps the reason I put Boers' book aside was that I couldn't imagine making such a journey at my age, not to mention so far from home.

After the Reformation, Protestant Christians, who had come to believe that God isn't limited to any given place, rejected the whole idea of pilgrimage. Some of us question the modern movement of walking a certain path, as saints have done in ages past. What we don't realize is that going to church or spending time in our prayer corner can be a pilgrimage too, that seeking God doesn't require arduous travel. As with every experience, the fruit is what you make of it. One of the authors Boers cites spoke of a marinating process, in which the pilgrim experience sits in its juices until it is ready to be cooked and shared with others.

Boers' article gave me an idea: Could the act of walking to my mailbox every day fit one definition of pilgrimage: "religiously motivated travel for the purpose of meeting and experiencing God with hopes of being shaped and changed by that encounter"? The author goes on to say that the kind of activity to which he is referring is a "concretely physical" spiritual practice. My own walks are both concrete and physical, and every step opens me to the possibility of an encounter with God. What my walks lack in length and ardor, they make up for in repetition. Daily. Every day on the way—like prayer: continual.

Another author who is cited by Boers, Brett Webb-Mitchell, made this point: "The importance of place in Christian faith shows that the honoring of place has ecological implications, and points the way to disciplines that integrate mind, body and spirit." Now I'm hooked. Of course this mundane walk down my long driveway is a pilgrimage.

"The importance of place in the Christian faith" rang like a bell calling me to worship right here on the prairie. Boers' comment that the "honoring of place has ecological implications" underscores the earthkeeping part of everything we do here. Webb-Mitchell points out that we don't misuse the place we love. I'm ready to admit that I never loved a patch of land more than this one. Before I began to fully embrace my life here on the prairie, the mountains seemed to be the only place to find God. Today I know that God sings to me every day right here, through nature and grace. The ecological implication is clear: Wherever God speaks is sacred ground.

Another Kind of Pilgrimage

"You've got to be kidding," exclaimed the young woman who checked me in to the college dorm and gave me my key. "You mean that women were never allowed to come until this year? That's really hard to believe!"

"Strange but true," was all I could think to say. Would she be interested in my story? Could she comprehend a place and a time when women were barred from attending the yearly denominational Synod because the majority of the all-male body believed that the Bible prohibited women from serving in the offices of the church? Would she believe that I and others like me had been journeying toward this day for more than thirty years? No, she couldn't and didn't.

Vervain

Some days I even find this hard to believe. For so many years when I was in Iowa in June at the summer workshop, one of my kids would call to break the bad news: "The guys voted women down again! Someone even suggested a five-year moratorium from talking about the issue." And then we'd cry together, until we'd decide it was silly to pay a phone bill for crying. After a week of seething, I'd pick myself up, dust myself off and start over again.

I never left my denomination, although others were more open to equality for women; tradition-minded people would not force me out of the church of my birth. On the opening day of the national meeting of Synod 2008, I walked into the meeting hall, to a space at the table with my name on it—one of the first women ever to serve this part of Christ's church as a delegate. This journey has not been for the fainthearted. Most of the women here had deflected many an outrageous sling or arrow from others who held contrary views, but together we pressed on. For now, both the hard road of this pilgrimage and arrival at the destination will have to marinate for a while before I can share their meaning for me.

The work of Synod was intense; I put home out of my mind both before and during the meetings. But as soon as the end was in sight, I couldn't wait to return home. Not just on account of the usual homing instinct but based also on the sure knowledge that I was missing a spectacular June show. When I left, the butterfly weed had been ready to burst open into glorious persimmon blooms. Had I missed its debut? Just imagine my awe when I pulled into the drive, after a week of churchly confinement, to a sea of orange.

Butterfly weed may be the greatest misnomer among wildflowers. Butterfly weed belongs to the family of milkweed, but each bush-like plant looks like a huge, rounded bouquet, quite unlike the plain stalk of milkweed. The blossoms last most of the summer, but when finally the petals fall little pods emerge on the stem, filled with winged seeds, just like those of their less flashy relations. The plants were hard to start, but those flying seedpods make sure now that they propagate swiftly. From a couple of small plants in the rain garden, they now dot our entire prairie.

I opened the window and sang to the flowers: "I am the church, you are the church, we are the church together…" I couldn't get enough of this open-air sanctuary, which put the whole historic Synod week in perspective: "But the LORD is in his holy temple, let all the earth be silent before him." (Habakkuk 2:20)

Postscript

Two gift days of soaking up the beauty of the prairie before I had to leave again. Months ago, when I realized that the National Synod and the Cathedral College Writing Workshop were back-to-back events, it was too late to cancel either. Not that I could have given up either the historic Synod or my chance to learn from Barbara Brown Taylor. What a juxtaposition: two firsts, one at the end of a tortuous journey and the other on the road to a life-giving journey of writing.

On the first day of the workshop I attended afternoon prayers in the magnificent Washington Cathedral. Musicians sang and chanted Psalm 34:19 (NRSV). "Many are the afflictions of the righteous, but the LORD rescues them from them all" were the perfect words to depict our long struggle, as women, for entry into the church's decision-making body. All we had wanted was a seat at the table. But the verse I later adopted for the week was "I sought the LORD, and he answered me; he delivered me from all my fears" (Psalm 34:4, emphasis added). In the end, it is only my own fear, not the decisions of the church, that prevent me from putting my deepest thoughts into words on paper. Yes, deliver me!

Yearly Pilgrimage

"When Moses came down from Mount Sinai…his face was radiant because he had spoken with the LORD." (Exodus 34:29)

Every year, after the long trip across the Great Plains to get to the mountains, I take a mountain pilgrimage. My family has come to expect—and respect—my self-centered declaration: no cooking, no babysitting, no obligations—today is mine. I don my hiking boots, comfortable clothes, and a baseball cap and grab my daypack with all I will need for my travels: a small notebook and pen, a New Testament, a rain jacket, extra socks, band-aids, lunch and a Diet Coke™.

My destination is another ghost town, Crystal City, seven miles up-mountain from Marble on a rough jeep road, which follows the river by the same name. Sometimes my husband talks me into a jeep-lift up the first steep mile, but I always slough off his "When will you be back?" with a flippant "Whenever."

On a weather-perfect day I share the road with mountain bikers, all-terrain vehicles, horses, jeeps and an occasional fellow hiker. The water beside me crashes and sloshes; birds and beasts chatter, scurry and rustle as I pass. I am hardly alone.

Religious pilgrimages are really a quest for God. I, like Moses, want to find him on the mountain. I want him to talk to me too; I want him to transform me. That will be no easy job. But the steady rhythm of my steps, mile after mile, has a way of opening my eyes as well as my ears. God and I meet and greet, mysteriously.

Sometimes it is near dusk when I descend the mountain and arrive back at the cabin, tired, sweaty, dirty—but always glowing.

Dear God, Thank you for meeting me where I am and for talking to me. Your voice whispers above the din of daily life—and makes me noticeably new. Amen.

Gentleman Apiarist

Nothing brings a dreamer down to earth faster than the sting of a bee. One day when Fritz was tending his beehives, I decided to photograph the photographer in his white suit, bonnet and gloves as he opened the hive and lifted off one of the "supers" to see if the bees had filled it with the good stuff. If full he would place another box with wax slats on the stack.

He approached the hives behind puffs of smoke that came from smoldering paper in a can with a top like a bellows. The worker bees will become mesmerized and docile and will lose the will to fight this potential robber dressed in white.

Fritz works fast because there are still plenty of angry bees hovering around. He's glad that he's even put duct tape around his ankles from pants to the tops of his shoes. He knows how angry they get when someone wants to take something they worked so hard to make. I stayed a healthy distance away, using the telephoto lens, but several bees spotted or smelled me and literally chased me back to the house. One bee was quicker than I and planted her stinger squarely on my jaw.

Inside the house, I fumbled for the remedies: baking soda paste, meat tenderizer and a tube that when broken

We only have to look at our verdant garden near Flat Iron Lake to know that our resident bees can take much of the credit."

Beekeeping at Flat Iron Lake

provides a fresh antidote on a swab. I called the beekeeper for help, as I could not see the stinger to pull it out. "They were really mad today!" said the white-clad man when he pulled the tiny black thread out with a tweezers. "I guess they took it out on the closest open flesh they could find. Does it hurt?"

The spot on the boney part of my jaw had already begun to swell. I am not dangerously allergic to stings but my body responds to all insect bites with a powerful histamine reaction. So after the stinging subsided, the evidence could not be hidden: a fat, sagging jaw that was

plants and insects, which is vital for growth. So often when we are picking raspberries with friends in the garden I have to assure them that all those bees working nearby will not hurt them. That didn't convince grandson, Matt, with fresh memories of being stung repeatedly by ground bees that he inadvertently stirred up. Honeybees have no interest in flesh when they are taking the nectar and pollen from your garden but only when you are trying to take it back from them in that nectar and chemical mixture we call honey.

Bees are such fascinating creatures. Their one-milligram-sized brain enables them to do complex tasks of navigation and communication. When one finds a source of nectar she can direct others to it by wiggling her body and giving directions based on the sun's position. The bees we see are "working girls" as one author noted, born to a single queen that rules the hive. Worker bees live only six weeks but the first three are used in hive-tasks before they are ready to hunt in wide-open spaces. Honeybees travel fast and far, helping pollinate plants and flowers in a huge radius. New research suggests that they have a photographic memory of flowers and landmarks.

beginning to turn blue-black. In the days that followed everyone asked, "What happened?" It took several months for the marble-sized knot to disappear.

I don't blame the bees—they do amazing work through-out the growing season, providing that necessary link between

Where are all the bees?

Fritz asked this simple question when traveling with development workers in Kenya. We had just passed white-topped, flowering acacia trees, known for the excellent honey that comes from their nectar. We soon learned about the traditional methods of beekeeping with hollowed logs positioned in the top of trees. The bees came and made their honey but harvesting it brought many challenges. Honey, wax and bee-parts came out together and could be filtered only with great difficulty. Raw honey was not pure honey.

The bees we could not see were everywhere—quietly doing their work. Not long after the innocent question, development workers researched and introduced modern hives to farmers desperate for a sustainable crop. In the Sugar Belt region of Kenya, beekeeping now flourishes. Enterprising people are managing the whole process from building hive bodies, to placing them for colonization, and then harvesting, extracting and bottling honey. The market for pure honey is vast and many "keepers," the majority of whom are women, can now support a whole family on the three harvests a year. Honey requires no special storage or preserving. It is nature's gift of nutrition, medicinal value and sweet enjoyment. Now it is also providing a living wage to many poor people in Africa.

Bees also remind us about the interconnectedness of life. For the last few years, scientist have puzzled over a bee disease that is claiming lots of colonies. For the first time many of us learned that even nuts like almonds need bees in their life cycle. We only have to look at our verdant garden near Flat Iron Lake to know that our resident bees can take much of the credit. Pausing with a sting on the jaw is the perfect time to say "Thanks, we couldn't have done it without you."

Winter Squash

Gardeners and cooks who work mainly with fresh vegetables must deal with lots of organic waste. The peels, the tough stalks of asparagus, the seeds in squash, and so much more must be discarded—but where? We know that they decompose over time and that throwing them in the trash makes for heavy lifting and inescapable waste. Country folk have almost always had their garbage piles (unless they owned pigs), but if they were too close to the house they stank and attracted foraging animals and bugs. Eventually, someone either had to plow the pile under or carry it away.

Many people want to compost their food scraps instead of putting them in the trash or down the garbage disposal. But composting is more than piling up veggie scraps. There's a science to it, especially if you intend to use the resulting compost for fertilizer in your garden. Somehow all that lumpy stuff must decompose or rot with the help of its own natural bacteria.

Composting is a burning process, so, just like fire, it needs a good supply of oxygen. If the pile of scraps is too dense, air can't get to the core, and the fire slows down. The necessary aeration must be achieved by turning, either manually or mechanically. One also needs both nitrogen (from grass clippings, coffee grounds, egg shells, uncooked vegetable waste and even hair trimmings) and carbon (from dead leaves, sawdust, chopped hay or straw, and even watered-down newsprint). If these two categories are balanced, the mix will turn to humus, which can later be used for fertilizer.

A recently developed method of composing uses earthworms. If the worms are placed in a container with food scraps, they eat the waste and leave as by-product a rich, dark, earth-smelling soil conditioner. Using this method is possible inside homes and during the winter. The vermicompost that results can be used for soil enrichment.

Learn more:

Worms Eat My Garbage by the late Mary Appelhof, an early pioneer of this method

"Compost and Its Moral Imperatives" in *Second Nature: A Gardener's Education* by Michael Pollan

Although we can never predict weather conditions and the
sequence of blooms from one year to the next,
July is the most reliable month for prairie splendor.

July Blooms

July is fullness: The fields rise up with petals and stalks reaching toward the light. Unless a path is kept open, no foot can find its way without having to thrash aside the hearty growth at every step. Hard going, as every square foot is crowded with life. And that is only the life we see. The underground ants, gophers, worms, ground hogs and seeds of yet-to-emerge plants represent alternate tracks of life we seem to step on with impunity. Besides what we see and know is hidden underground, more life thrives unseen—except with a microscope. Even the air is full, which isn't evident until the ragweed gets our allergies going. In July we see the landscape topping out, packed as full as it can be this growing season.

July is the prairie's pinnacle. As Scripture puts it, "the fullness of his grace we have all received one blessing after another." (John 1:16) This scene is a hint of that kind of fullness and blessing, stretching as far as my eye can see. Jake and I walk on the mowed path until an unexpected movement of foliage catches our attention. It may be a snake slithering along the ground. Jake pounces repeatedly, like a cat, but the reptile is too fast for him. We continue past the beehives, careful not to get in the "beeline" and interrupt the route of bee to hive with its nectar. A few days ago Fritz removed the top two supers off the hive—they were almost too heavy to lift.

Friends like to come out when the prairie is full. Several years ago we offered a "picnic on the prairie" as a fund-raiser at an auction for our local school. High interest brought in a tidy sum and started a tradition of July prairie picnics. Although we can never predict weather conditions and the sequence of blooms from one year to the next, July is the most reliable month for prairie splendor. One day I got a call from someone we had met briefly at a meeting who was now camping with relatives at nearby Wabasis Lake. His group had heard about the prairie and wondered whether a few of them could come and see it. Before we knew it, ten people had piled out of two cars. This July is so lovely we want everyone to see and enjoy the wildflowers.

I am spending delightful afternoons in my garden watching everything living around me. As I grow older, I feel everything departing and I love everything with more passion.

Emile Zola

A Sudden Summer Storm

"High summer," some would call it. But wonder and delight in growing things can't rid my memory of a natural disaster that visited our family one July. It was the summer of 1981, the same one that saw us in transition from East Lansing to Cleveland. Our son Doug was at his own pinnacle. He had graduated from high school and was to enter college after a summer job at a Lake Michigan resort. His zest for living matched that of the heartiest of plants, like the big bluestem or the black-eyed Susan. He pushed forward his tall, lanky frame as self-assured and independent as the fourth of July.

We got the call on the loveliest of July days: A dive into shallow water from a water ski, a broken neck, a paralyzed body. I try not to dwell on the horrors of that day or the year of hospitalization that followed. I will my mind to let go of the decades of problem solving, barriers and heartaches that have complicated his life. Rather, I see him still in fullness and as independent as any quadriplegic can be. His own declaration of independence is evidenced by his determination to be a good father to his three children and a steadfast husband to Mary. With a master's degree in social work, he spends his days in a grade school setting with children who gravitate to him just as he is. Fullness has many faces.

But anniversaries catch us short. Every twelfth of July we pause to remember the day and event that changed us forever. That day, over twenty years ago, led to a season in my life in which God's fullness seemed as depleted as a helium balloon already descending from the ceiling. My first journal entry following the accident:

Journal Entry

7/21/81–The tragedy has immobilized us. All of living has become unimportant and senseless. Existence is measured from hour to hour, and its worth by how Doug feels. When the going gets rough, we cannot pretend. We are frightened for him and for ourselves. We cannot bear his pain, but it still weighs us down. Comfort—if he is comfortable we relax just a little and look up at the sky and comment on the weather. If there is pain, we cannot see the sun, even if it is shining.

Back to the present: Doug and I do a lot of remembering; we're trying to write a book about his life. He is blessed or cursed with a memory that brings back every face, color, indignity, laugh and passion that have made up his forty-five years. One day each week I leave Flat Iron Lake and travel the forty-five minutes to his house to work on the book. Progress is slow; specific memory gets in the way as we roar over some devious prank he never told me about or find ourselves unable to hold back the tears in remembering how hard it was for him to make that first date from the seat of a wheelchair. Too often there are glitches with his voice-activated computer. Some days just evaporate—days when the top priority isn't on writing but on getting an adjustment on his wheelchair or having new hand splints made. In the end, we're determined to make ours a hopeful book.

We hear about natural disasters on the news, and we have certainly felt the brunt of this one. God's providence, incomprehensible in the face of bad things like Doug's accident, takes on an added dimension here at Flat Iron Lake, where living things seems so orderly and predictable. I think back only four months to the prairie burn in April that charred this land and devastated every living thing within reach of the licking flames. Now there is fullness of life everywhere. God's abiding presence is on display in the lives of those that were once brought low. "As long as the earth endures, seedtime and harvest, cold and heat, summer and winter, day and night will never cease." (Genesis 8:22)

Garden Watch | *Waiting for buds to bloom*

My husband gardens as a master; he may never have been certified by a garden club as Master Gardener, but his talent is legendary. I relish the blooms and the fruit and the good things his work bring to my eyes and to my mouth. But if he were an amateur gardener like me, he'd understand my lack of calculation and precision. He does not. I had thought it was enough to plant and wait for my buds to bloom.

Take my geraniums in planters on the deck. Every year since we lived here we've purchased the same kind from the same vendor. However, this year they were out of this kind on the day we were there. Rather than driving the considerable distance back, I went to an open-air market close by and purchased the very same type. I cleaned the large wooden pots, replaced some soil, and carefully replanted the geraniums alongside a few others: spikes as background, dusty miller to fill in between the green, and miniature pansies for groundcover. I watered them twice but then forgot them for a few days while attending some important meetings.

When I returned and checked, some full red blooms had faded. I snipped them off and watered all the plants to encourage growth in other drooping new heads. They never did stand up straight and soon just dried up. Of course, the master had a good deal of advice, but by then it was too late. He forecast disaster and concluded that I'd purchased the cheap kind of geranium instead of the ever-blooming variety. I protested. His verdict was that the only thing I could do was let them go this year.

So I asked my green-thumb sister, a master in her own right, for advice. She was gentler—accepting the presenting problem without dredging up history. Add some liquid fertilizer, water every day because of the intense summer sun on the deck for half the day, and be diligent about deadheading.

I became more attentive, feeling as though I had to hand-deliver the nourishment so my wee ones would grow. In order to keep an eye on them, I turned the patio table into my writing desk. I kept a full watering can at the ready. Meanwhile, the breezes blew, waving the White Birch next to me; the birds called each other and included me; and the clouds swirled above, changing shape each time I looked. And in time new buds formed.

I am waiting for the proof that even I can nurture life. Geranium buds come in clusters, some more than a dozen strong. Each plant brings forth three or four clusters at a time. The first glint of red appears to announce the commencement of summer life for my plants in their new home on our deck. I sit and wait as each, with agonizing slowness, breaks out from its green covering—in contrast to the fast-frame moving picture I've seen of the blooming desert.

This waiting game excites me. Not by its action but by it relentless slow motion. I cannot stop growth now, unless I pluck the plants from the ground. They don't know how they have vindicated me. This time I've proved my husband wrong but have in the process learned a valuable lesson: Care requires more than checking in once in a while. Plants, like children, demand a continuous watchful eye. So now, like an attentive midwife, I sit watching and waiting for all those pregnant buds to give birth.

Garden Watch | *Naming*

The numbers are growing—you'd think we were offering free beer or tickets to an amusement park. Cyclists interrupt their long-distance treks to fill their water bottles and have a look. A friend wonders whether he can bring Aunt Suzie, who was quite a gardener in her day. And after an article appeared in the gardening section of the local paper, garden clubs called to set a date to come and see our wildflowers and grasses in bloom. Sharing is fun, until someone asks, "What's the name of that flower?" Innocent question. Suddenly I become the naturalist I have no right to call myself. Our flowers are wildflowers—even avid gardeners can't identify some blooms. With so many types, I often stumble on names. Since Fritz and I are out there together and his recall sometimes falters, he turns it over to me: "Carol is much better with names than I am."

Thanks, but that just makes the burden heavier. Couldn't we have isolated just a few plants for quick viewing? Why not put out markers, as the botanical gardens do? No. Each spring I put myself through a remedial identification course. Two or three guidebooks in hand, I try to match flowers and grasses to pictures, so as to learn their proper names. I keep lists, draw primitive sketches, and try to stay ahead of an abundance of new sightings every day. I want to be ready for the inevitable snap quiz, by naming aloud each flower as I pass. But when that next person asks the name question, I'm never sure I'll get the answer right.

I don't want to be their guide. Naming seems to squelch other kinds of wondering and particularity. If I were their teacher, I'd want them to look closely at the petals, stamens, and shape and arrangement of leaves. I've been threatening to turn the question around to, "What kind of flower do you think that is? Here are the books that helped me identify it; see whether you can find it." So much more fun, and such an effective teaching method.

I'd really like to assemble a book of sketches of the most common flowers and grasses and allow folks to discover for themselves. But, of course, at the end of the growing season I always find another priority and lay that one aside. We've got a couple of sketching grandchildren—maybe I'll invite them to a summer camp at our place with their only job being to sketch what they see for inclusion in my little book. This would help all of us look more closely.

If Fritz hadn't shown me the subtle difference between invasive Canadian goldenrod and the stiff goldenrod by the way their leaves are attached to the stems, I couldn't have culled the bad ones from the rain garden. That gives me an idea: I'll tell anyone who wants to enjoy the prairie that there's a price—a little sweat equity. I'll supply the gloves and show them where the bad guys live and how to identify them—and then tell them that one pail full of junk plants gets you an admission to see the prized ones.

The Invasives

The cosmic battle between good and evil is being played out right here on the prairie. And like many such clashes, it's not always easy to tell the good guys from the bad. As every gardener knows, some weeds are beautiful, even though they will eventually choke out the flowers or the vegetables that are supposed to be in their spot. Prairie restorers call them "the invasives." The majestic thistle is one great big bad guy. If we'd let him, he'd grow as tall as a tree and plant a large family all around him.

The thistle—and here I use the generic rather than the specific name—doesn't flower until late summer. The bloomheads are like miniature pineapples with fuchsia tops. If you wait for color, the propagation has already taken place. To preempt them, one must search for their distinctive, deep-cut, spiky leaves. They're easy to spot from the driveway because of the darker, more substantive foliage, but unlike some bad guys you can't just grab and pull upward, or the thistle will leave your hand bloodied. Occasionally I have tried to pull out a seedling at its base with one hand, trying to steer clear of the thorny leaves. It seldom works. I need leather gloves and a sharp shovel, not items I generally carry with me on my walk.

A distance from the drive, they grow undisturbed until someone feels their sharpness against bare legs. Some rise over six feet in height—soon visible in any crowd. Their pineapple heads are loaded with seeds that will soon be looking for a place of their own in which to burrow.

Thistles are only one invasive species. It seems that when land was cleared for other uses, opportunistic plants took over. I soon heard the names vetch and crown vetch, spoken in tones one might reserve for "the Mafia," with reference to the opportunists that have taken over every inch of the banks along the roadways. Briefly during the summer, they glow a beautiful rose or lavender, looking like a plush carpet. But they are up to no good. Spreading underground in a sinister fashion, they dominate fields, preventing other species from securing a "ground hold."

We didn't know just how many invasives there were until after we had tried to plant native species. The corn or soybeans, which had alternated for years on the land before our arrival, didn't seem to mind a few weeds. They were harvested along with the crops and became cattle fodder. But when new seeds tried to take hold, the invasives asserted themselves to defend their territory. Each week there seemed to be a newcomer.

We mobilized. With each new enemy we formed a posse. I was the sentry, watching for them as I walked the drive, once Fritz had shown me which plants to hate. Then he'd come out to get them. But once I was sensitized to identifying the bad plants, I saw them everywhere. Finally, he begged me to go after them too. Only one catch: You had to pull them and rid them from the land. My trips to the mailbox elongated, as I stopped, pulled and piled invasives along the route. Like Eliot Ness, I spotted the enemy everywhere.

A friend wanted to bring a visitor out to see the prairie. "Do you have Queen Anne's lace?" she bubbled. "I just love

them." "Not if we can help it!" was my brusque reply. They had become my latest must-pulls. I found it hard to explain why this elegant, complex, lacy bloom that waves so airily in the breeze would have to be banished. Only those of us who have pulled them know about their long, carrot-like root.

Uprooting invasives has become like a game. Once I got beyond the fact that this was not the way I wanted to spend my time in nature, I became like a microbe hunter. Weeds resembled an opportunistic cancer that had to be destroyed. Fritz has always been a gardener, as well as a scientist, who knows that there is a best time for certain chores. I would have preferred to wait for pleasant, not-too-hot weather, when the ground was moist. But this luxury was not to be. "We've got to get them before…" Whatever word he used, it was framed as a now-or-never proposition. This creeping plague could ruin the whole prairie.

Sometimes when tired, I reasoned that we were the invasives—we people who came with good intentions of restoring something precious but ended up destroying the very plants that had squatters' rights. They, after all, were here first, so what right have I to send them packing? But the lecture had been given, and it would be given again: Restoration means returning the land to its natural state. My sense of history wasn't long enough. But could we really go back to the beginning?

One night as we walked just for fun, I saw a magnificent thistle with a deep purple top. My learned response was to go back to get the shovel, but Fritz stopped me, surrendering to fairness and eye-appeal. "We don't have to eliminate every last one—they're just too beautiful." Occasionally the gardener's heart softens and the bad guy wins.

SIGHTINGS | *The Circle of Life*

Our grandchildren are outgrowing their once-favorite video, *The Lion King.* I remember when I had to watch it with them because some parts were just too scary to them. There was, after all, this predator problem: Some beasts waited to pounce on other beasts—usually little, defenseless lion cubs that had let their curiosity take them to places their parents had forbidden them to go. The jackals with their teeth barred required a fast-forward, especially for the youngest two, Dani and Morgan. Walking in the woods, I had chosen to hide the feathers of the dead swan baby from sight. I wanted to protect the girls from unpleasant scenes in nature.

But now, with all their first-grade maturity, they understand that *The Lion King* is only a movie, not real life. But they have also spotted that featherless baby robin, lying dead beside the path, and been scolded for stepping on the rare pink lupine in the field. Dead things don't reproduce; the circle of life is broken.

When did I put aside my idyllic view of nature? Before moving to this place I had enjoyed a car-window view of the environment and its operation. In the world of plants, we expect seasonal growth, flowering and dying. It's so natural and predictable. The life of many plants continues, however, even after they die back and lie unresponsive for months. Given the right conditions, they rise again and begin a new life-cycle phase. Not so with animals. We pet lovers accept that animals have a life span that is generally shorter than that of humans. Children raise a puppy as a member of the family but are then forced to watch him grow older, at a rate faster than their own, a pace so accelerated that they often lose the pet before they themselves have left the family home. From a moving car or even on a hike through a nature preserve, the circle of life isn't on display. But walking down the driveway I nearly step on the dead bodies of voles or hurry past the stench of a woodchuck carcass rotting in the ditch.

Predator and Prey

Sometimes I even watch predators at their work. One day I saw what looked like an upright green stick near the edge of the drive. A few yards away I recognized it as a praying mantis. Within a foot, I could see that the mantis was holding in his skinny fingers the upper leg of a grasshopper, still attached to its body, and chewing it as though it were a drumstick. The pray-er had become the prey-er, and his strange head with its bulging eyes so top-heavy on his skinny body noticed me not at all. I wasn't invited to his picnic.

Fritz's camera recorded another predator in action: a snake grabbing a frog, also on the upper thigh, when the two confronted each other in the grass behind our house. The picture shows both the predator's gleaming eye and the frog's leg and arm extended with eyes alert, as though registering that he nearly got away. And maybe he did. Had the snake opened its mouth to maneuver the big, one-bite meal down the hatch, the frog might have wiggled away, despite having been mortally wounded. In my mind I know that every animal has to eat; in my heart I don't want to believe that they eat each other.

"Out of sight, out of mind," the old saying goes, and it's certainly true out here on the lake. A summer research student is doing an aquatic inventory of the lake: plants, fish and fowl. Since I rarely swim in the lake anymore, my knowledge is limited to what I can see on the surface: waxy water lily pads, dotted with balls of white or yellow flowers; bluegills and an occasional bass on the end of a fisherman's line; and, waterfowl, such as Canadian geese, mute swans and ducks, trailed as they are during the early days of the warm season by goslings, ducklings and cygnets.

There is the occasional sighting of the beaver, but mostly in early spring. I hear the twangy sound of bullfrogs in the evening, but it's so easy to forget about other amphibians. The turtles show themselves only when they labor up the hill in June to lay their eggs in some sandy spot. The next morning, when only broken eggshells mark the spot, I promptly forget about the snapping turtles. Until, that is, the numbers of baby water birds plunge noticeably downward. Before I can even get a good look at the swan babies, there are only two. I wouldn't miss one of the goslings trailing its parents, who, in my opinion, should really get serious about family planning. But the swans are precious.

"Weren't there four babies; I only see two!" I remark to the ecology student. "I think the snapping turtle got the other two," he replied matter-of-factly. "When they're small, they're the perfect meal for the old turtle." Suddenly, I imagine turtles everywhere, ready to sidle up to newborn waterfowl and bite off a foot or devour the whole bird. That same day Bruce called to announce the birth of two sets of Mallard ducks, one with three and the other with seven. I already fear for those little ones that may become a turtle's morning snack. I'm glad I don't have to watch.

Nature Watch | *Fleabane*

In the past, my work tied me to my computer screen and
away from the window. But my new laptop is moveable, and
someti⋯ the scene just beyond both distracts and attracts
me⋯. A sea of white greets me, and because of a
⋯ea is filled with breakers so thick there is
⋯ween them. The new white sea fills
⋯that has dogged us for years; it
⋯roduce the wild grasses and
⋯grow. The little blue-
⋯s invasive weeds are
⋯new tenants? Thou-

⋯are four- or six-legged pests
⋯bite some of us unmercifully,
⋯are plants, not animals (although
⋯ward off fleas). Fleabane is a daisy-
⋯ch across, with hundreds of white
⋯w center. Each plant has about twenty-
five ⋯ney cluster with thousands of others of their
kind to ⋯ area. "Are they bad guys?" I ask Fritz, knowing that if they are, I'll be pulling for the rest of the summer.

Any time I see too much of one kind of flower, I'm immediately convinced they'll be as troublesome as the purple-
or rose-colored vetch that have invaded the roadway medians
and ditches. His demeanor, however, assures me that the
invasion of the fleabane doesn't worry him. "Next spring when

Fleabane

we burn this section, the fleabane will recede and the little blue with their long roots will thrive." A long-range perspective always helps.

Looking at them again, I remember what one biologist said while visiting: "I can't understand why folks plant, water and cut green grass. It does nothing but stand up straight. It has no motion or life to call attention to itself." For someone who loves and studies plants, it's important to understand them as living, moving beings. I'm reminded that the phrase from an old hymn, "In the rustling grass I hear him pass," must have referred to native grasses because bluegrass doesn't rustle; it just stands at-attention, uniform green. The warm-season grasses aren't yet very tall, so I'm glad to be positioned to witness the waving sea of fleabane—speaking its life-language in today's soft and silently moving air.

Coda:

On the last day of July, three flowers seemed to beg me to immortalize them on paper: the common mullein, the hoary alyssum, and the purple vervain. They couldn't be more distinct from one another. The mullein is that tall, single stalk, thick as my thumb, that sprouts small yellow flowers on its head. It has mint-green, furry leaves near its base. Just when you think you've discovered the first of the season, its brothers and sisters rise like sentries all across the field.

The white hoary alyssum may take the prize for longevity, as it was among the first of summer and is still growing strong. The alyssum plant is close to the ground and not at all showy, but its many stalks, all protruding from one base, have a perpetually flowery end. When I pass, I think of a certain fourth-of-July firework—the one that invisibly shoots up high, bangs, and then sends many runners from one spot, which in turn brighten at the end of their flight and then pop again. But unlike the night show that fades before our eyes, the alyssum keeps growing and that glowing end—all summer long.

And then there's purple vervain that resembles miniature candelabra gathered around one main stalk above a leafy stem. Vervain, with its delicate and startling violet coat made up of clusters of tiny blooms, attracts photographers, while the mullein is noticed primarily because finches like to perch on its top, surveying the territory.

All three of these flowers sprout minute clusters of snap-dragon-like blooms, but unlike most wildflowers that blossom, fade and go to seed, these flowers creep upward on their stalks, leaving seed pods beneath as they continue to grow and flower above. No wonder I'm partial to these guys—they never seem to die.

Every Cloud Has One

"Be joyful always; pray continually; give thanks in all circumstances, for this is God's will for you in Christ Jesus."
(1 Thessalonians 5:16–18)

"Look for the silver lining whenever clouds appear in the blue. Remember somewhere the sun is shining,"
I loved to croon with Perry Como.

Not until I got the sweatshirt that Christmas did I realize what a Pollyanna I had been. "Every Cloud Has A Silver Lining," it read, and the gift-givers got a good laugh when they saw my face as I held it up and read the inscription. My gift with a message came from a sister-in-law and brother-in-law with whom my husband and I had partnered to build a prefab cottage by Lake Michigan. Through all the ups and downs of our shoestring project, the variable lake weather, and our combined seven kids—I must have played the role of eternal optimist, always trying to see the bright side. I suppose I should either credit or blame my mother, who modeled that silver-lining attitude all her life.

But that eternal optimism got me trouble. When things are bad, they said and I agree today, don't call them good. When life gets hard here on Earth, don't pacify me with talk of a perfect heaven by-and-by. It doesn't help to spiritualize the awful. I remember laughing when a pastor told of his neighbor lady, who had shared with him about her broken refrigerator, which had spoiled all her food and left a dripping, stinky mess. At that point she had dutifully praised the Lord. At least in front of the preacher.

I don't bother my friends and family with trite optimism any longer—especially after all the trying things that have happened in my life. Each of us has to put our dark clouds in perspective, in our own time and style. But I'm still fascinated by God's hopeful sky-signs. I look for the bright and silvery rim on dark clouds when they pick up sunlight from somewhere away from, or above, the storm. And the thin night clouds drifting past the moon on an otherwise dark night. Their amazing beauty is enough to remind me that black clouds come and go but that they do not spoil my fair-weather plans forever.

Dear God,
Thank you for hope, especially when everything looks dark. May I find better ways in which to be your silver lining to others.
Amen.

Thistle

Whether we call them exotics, aliens, or just bad guys, the message is clear: They don't belong here. Native prairies need native plants, the ones that are indigenous to their region. But other plants have immigrated to the area, and the longer they stay the more naturalized they will become. Only when we burn an area do the long-rooted, especially-suited-to-this-land-and-climate plants begin to emerge once again.

The immigrants linger; they don't want to move. They have established themselves in the area by hearty propagation, which makes our job so much more difficult. Larger patches of invasive plants like crown vetch can be sprayed with Roundup™, which will kill them without harm to the environment, but most invasives stand side-by-side with native plants and must be plucked out, one by one. The larger your section of prairie to restore, the more daunting the job becomes.

First, you must be able to identify flowering plants in order to sort the good from the bad. Bad plants can be incredibly beautiful and rich in color. They often prefer to camouflage themselves by sidling up to native plants of similar color. Once you've trained yourself to tell them apart, you must pull or dig them up by the roots. Some begin to propagate quickly (think dandelion), so there is only a small window of pulling time. Purple vetch drapes itself among and through grasses and soon manufactures hearty seedpods. Wild carrot or Queen Anne's lace has deep roots and abundant seeds in its broad flowers. Curly dock, which turns deep maroon when mature, produces hundreds of unwanted seeds per stalk. When hoary alyssum (the one that fascinated me in June) began to propogate wildy, I realized it was also on the invasive list in Michigan.

Native prairies are natural, but keeping them that way calls for uncommon vigilance by their caretakers. Fire helps, but weeding out, one by one, is the most effective long-term defense against those stubborn invasives.

Learn more:

National Arboretum – www.usna.usda.gov/invasive
Michigan Invasive Plant Council (MIPC) –
http://invasiveplantsmi.org

Fritz taught me to look for crow's feet tips

as a sure sign of big bluestem.

One early morning when the night rain still hung on the

plants, I saw a whole field of big blue.

Did they spring up overnight, skipping adolescence

altogether to their amazing mature height?

Big Bluestem

August brings a different kind of fullness. All summer I observed that the vegetation on one side of the drive was much shorter than that on the other. The pale violet bee balm grew thick and tall on the side bounded by woods, while milkweed and butterfly weed dotted rather than dominated the other side. I assumed that the April burn had slowed their growth. But by August the tall grasses on the lakeside, which had also been burned, rose taller than my head. Where had they been all summer? Was I so busy looking at color that I hadn't see them?

Fritz taught me to look for crow's feet tips as a sure sign of big bluestem. One early morning when the night rain still hung on the plants, I saw a whole field of big blue. Did they spring up overnight, skipping adolescence altogether to their amazing mature height? While thinking about the mystery, I came upon yet another prairie book, this one with sketches of flowers and grasses, the kind I had thought of asking the grandkids to draw. Browsing, I found my bluestem answer:

"Prairie grasses grow down, not up. The root system establishes itself first before the grass appears... Big bluestem roots have been known to be 12 feet long. Leaves will curl in dry, windy weather so that less area is exposed, conserving the moisture in the leaf. Roots store starch as food for the plant...if there has been a dry season, the plant will take time to renourish itself before it is able to use the energy for making flowers, fruit and seeds... the above ground growth tissues of grass is located toward the base of the plant rather than the tip." (Shirley Shirley) I can only imagine the soil under the surface filled with those deep roots, well placed to prevent erosion.

Come forth in the light of things, let nature be your teacher.

William Wordsworth

Now the burning makes sense—not that it kept down growth but that it has encouraged colossal growth in the very plants we hoped to restore. And while I was neither looking at nor tending them, the wild grasses flourished. Now with my new guide in hand, I begin to identify the types of grasses. The naming job should be much easier than it is with flowers because there are only five main warm-weather grasses. I think my memory bank can hold that many. However, in the fullness of August they seem to be the same color brown, so they demand closer observation. Little bluestem plants stand about a foot-and-a-half tall and line the drive on both sides, low enough so that the flowers beyond can be seen. They are the same grass clumps that looked like green and black porcupines soon after the burn. At maturity they begin to put out feathery seeds that can be harvested by grabbing a few stalks and the base and pulling toward you. As tiny as they are, they soon fill a paper lunch bag.

The wild grass called Canadian rye resembles a grain plant like wheat. Its heavy head curves the end of the stem and often waves in the wind. Indian grass grows one cluster of seedpods out of each tubular stem. Straight and tall, the plant's pods are shaped like a skinny Christmas tree and soon swell with teeny yellow ornaments dangling from each branch. The petals drop quickly, but the tree remains and turns the most amazing bronze as fall approaches. Switch grass, which startled me with its frozen beauty last January, looks delicate with its slight, stiff stalks. As it grows, the itty-bitty branches level horizontally with amazing toughness that belies their size.

Now back to big bluestem—the king of the prairie. All native grasses have long roots, but this one outdoes them all. Like the biggest NBA player, he has a good "understanding" and dominates the play. Those little crow's feet that make big blue easy to identify soon dangle tiny seedpods from their undersides. They intend to be fathers of a great nation, with children as many as the sands of the seashore. Having what the psalmist called a "quiver…full of them" (Psalm 127:5) is enough to bring happiness to any man, beast or plant.

August 28, 2005
Birthday Blues

One late summer day each year starts out as others before it. I notice its light, heat and character as I slip out the backdoor with Jake for his morning walk. He sniffs some bushes and tree trunks before picking one, as I walk down the sloping driveway toward the barn. Each morning my senses grab one color or form or sound for closer attention. But this day, my meandering mind gets stuck on one thing: The day is supposed to be special. After all, it's my birthday.

Did I expect all nature to sing just for me today? The wildflowers wobble in the breeze just as they did yesterday; the birds sing to each other, taking no notice of me. The dog begs for morning biscuits—he has no gift for me. Even my husband rushes out early, without a word, to help at the local hunger center.

Most days loom large with possibilities—a perpetual invitation. They have no weight or freight when they dawn, just a slate upon which I'm permitted to write. The marks I make are often less than hoped for, but the days, like pages, pile up and take shape. Eventually, night forces me to turn out the light on the last words of others from books and magazines stacked beside my bed. Over time, both life and work seem to make sense.

Not so on August 28—the day of my birth. Its coming does not surprise or horrify me. The years, numbering more than sixty now, have been sweet, not full of remorse or regret.

The problem is just the day—twenty-four hours of trying to mark this day as special.

Birthdays of my youth meld together as a recurring scenario. I was the second born of five children—the first three of us with birthdays within one week's time. Mine came first on the calendar. My busy mother, who always carried more than her share of the weight of family life, wasn't big on birthday celebrations. The youngest of twelve children, she herself couldn't recall a single party to mark her own birthday. Nevertheless, on mine I always hoped for a special day, one entirely devoted to me. Instead, I was just one of the brood, with a mouth to feed and clothes to be mended. On my day I became a quiet, brooding, disappointed little girl. Finally, when someone asked "What's wrong with Carol?" I'd have my chance to blurt, "It's my birthday—and no one even cares!" "Oh, my, you're right," my mom would say, always apparently surprised. "We'll have to bake a cake to celebrate all your birthdays." I can't remember longing for gifts—I just wanted to be noticed for no other reason than my birthday self. But lumping my day with my brother and sister's birthdays just didn't cut it.

Only one birthday stands out during my childhood—the August 28 when I turned ten. Earlier in the summer I had gotten my first glasses, which opened up a new, clearer world to me. The week before school began we joined another family on a rare trip to the mountains—near a famous trout stream. The gang fussed over me—the birthday girl. Then my Dad, usually an introspective, serious man, invited me to come fishing with him. The afternoon began joyfully but ended in near tragedy when Dad had to rescue me from drowning in the Canejos River. I might have blanked out that memory, were it not for two black-and-white photographs memorializing the day: the first of some happy children eating cake and drinking soda from glass bottles, and the second of a bedraggled birthday girl who had tried to cross through the swift current just to meet her father at the appointed time.

I married a man whose birthdays, like mine, had passed without hoopla. But with our own children I tried to set a new standard. Our three were also born close to one another on the calendar—one each at the beginning, middle and last day of August. Whatever flair I lacked for party-making, I still hoped to make each feel special.

Moms always know their own birthday has little significance to their children, but perhaps, like me, grow more hopeful as those children become parents and party planners themselves. I made a fuss over my husband's sixtieth birthday, but when mine came—nothing. I boldly informed them all a few years ago that I was highly sentimental about my birthday. Forget Mother's Day or Christmas, I begged; those are days when one is acknowledged for being a good mom or a member of the family. I suppose I have always been looking for a celebration of me, without any particular merit, just for being me.

Somehow all the wrong people seem to remember my birthday—investment specialists, insurance agents, and even a hardware store, from which I receive cards jauntily signed by all the employees, none of whom cares anything about this particular me. But I leave the cards lying around in conspicuous places in the hope that others might notice.

This year the old birthday blues came out in multicolor. On Saturday I walked down the long driveway to our rural mailbox, knowing that one familiar card would not be there. Despite her earlier history with birthdays, Mom never forgot mine or anyone else's within the family. A small card, usually the kind you get free from the Paralyzed Veterans, always arrived on time with a $10 bill tucked inside, long after that amount of money bought only a modest lunch. Her devotion to my day was firm. Her death last year ended that long tradition.

I pulled down the mailbox door to find only one piece of mail. It was a duplicate, exuberant card from the insurance company with the same configuration of signatures. I wanted to stomp on it.

Well, if no card, then my children will surely call. I waited. One brother did call from Tennessee—his jovial voice on the answering machine wishing me a happy one but reminding me that his birthday follows mine by one day. An hour before dinnertime I broke the silence, reminding my husband that we usually go out for dinner on my birthday. He was chagrined but quickly acted as though he'd been planning to go out all along.

Sunday was quiet. Monday I walked to the mailbox expectantly, sure that my birthday cards had just been

delayed in the mail. Tuesday. Wednesday. And then the frantic calls—each kid hoping the others had remembered on time. "Don't worry," I say in my most self-assured, motherly voice, "I've decided to skip my birthday next year and enjoy all of the 364 wonder-filled days in between."

Thinking about Mortality

To fight off encroaching age, or the perception of aging during the month of my seventieth birthday, I've decided to walk for an hour three days a week. An hour, with no backtracking, takes me from my door, down the drive and around our rural block: Hart to Wabasis to Ten Mile to Lessiter and back again to Hart. It's a pleasant walk on pavement, up and down hills and beside orchards. This is my neighborhood, and what it lacks in human neighbors is more than compensated in nature's variety. Sometimes I walk with my I-pod running an episode of "Speaking of Faith," but often I'm just deep in thought in the early morning.

I wouldn't have to walk an hour to stay in shape—the experts say thirty minutes is good enough. But after my first long walk I realize there are other benefits as well. For one, I see and hear things I've missed before. One day I heard a splash beside the road that could only have been made by a large animal. I realized for the first time that a small pool lay just beyond the guardrail, shrouded by bushes and vines.

Along the road on the other side of Flat Iron Lake I saw a post with signs offering ducks and chickens—the same birds that greet me every morning with their cackling and crowing. Then, as I rounded the turn onto my drive, a group of four sandhill cranes lifted their long, skinny bodies into flight, croaking loudly as they passed overhead. I think two are slightly smaller—this year's offspring? My final observation was that unused land will quickly be overrun with invasive, but lovely, Queen Anne's lace. Soon the flowering heads will roll into tennis-sized, feathery balls packed full of seeds, to be carried far and wide.

On today's walk I remember my dad. In terms of longevity, I like to think of my mother's long and healthy life; one always hopes to resemble the long-lived one. But as my birthday approaches, I think more of Dad, who died within weeks of his own seventieth birthday. I suppose he knew he was living on the edge because of several heart attacks and a poor prognosis at the M.D. Anderson Clinic in Texas. But he worked as though he were still vibrant—and he was, intellectually. He couldn't think about retirement—said he didn't know what he'd do with himself. Had he read all the books he wanted to read? Had he seen the places he'd dreamed of when he was combing those magazines his rural neighbor shared with him—that farm boy with big ideas? Had he strengthened ties with old friends and with his own children?

Did he sense God's presence during those last years? I'll never know. He was a visionary who at one point stopped dreaming and began looking back on the accomplishments of his life. He found them inadequate. He traveled far but had no desire to roam. As for relationships, he didn't or couldn't bring himself to venture into any new territory or to examine the past, with its joys or failures. My own attempts were thwarted repeatedly, and then Doug's accident zapped my energy for taking an active role in bringing us together. I wish I had pressed. And then I think of my own children, at the same mid-forty place where I had been at that time, and wonder who ever really thinks their parent will die. What testimony of God's faithfulness is my life to them?

The last time I was with Dad was in the fall of 1981, when he and Mom came to Cleveland for the first time to see Doug in the hospital. Dad called and wrote often, but when he saw our situation firsthand, he went into his more comfortable action mode. He made his own professional assessment of Doug in the hospital and then made calls to other doctors who had spinal cord patients, even engaging in a lengthy phone conversation with a quadriplegic from Florida. The result for him was a sense of hopelessness for Doug's life going forward. He couldn't hide it. When he and Mom left, I felt worse than before they had come. Dad revealed a depression about his own life and about that of his grandson as well.

When my siblings made plans to meet our parents in Colorado that Christmas, I knew it was out of the question for us—we couldn't leave Doug that long. But neither could I muster the fortitude or desire to make the trip. Now I see the pictures of that holiday event, the last snapshots of my dad before his fatal heart attack. He was the same age I am now. The sad and serious image of him brings tears to my eyes. Not only because he died but because he didn't pass on in peace.

None of us is ready to die at seventy, or maybe ever. But Dad's expression on those last photos reminds me how much I want to live—until I die. I've heard it said that dying of cancer has some advantages; it gives you a little time to put things right. But not knowing how death will come for me, I try to imagine my reaction to a prognosis of only six months more. I'd read more books and talk about their ideas with others. I'd decide which pieces of my writing are worth editing and preserving. I'd work on relationships with all the important people in my circle and even try to form new ones.

Today, I'll talk to God as I walk around the block and seek his wisdom about how to enjoy all the days he gives me. Today, and every day, I'll beg for his presence and peace. "When we walk with the Lord…what glory he sheds on our way." (Trust and Obey)

August, 2008 – On Strike

My husband is going away, in the heat of summer in the fullness of the garden, in the height of the harvest season. He needs to pack for the trip to Alaska but is preoccupied by what he's leaving behind. Long to-do lists and long workdays have always marked his pre-vacation preparations. He has trouble letting go—his house must be in order. But this year I'm staying behind—fishing with five guys for ten days held zero appeal—so his lists, priorities and worries are being transferred to me, want them or not. What I do want is a retreat from meal planning, his schedule, and getting home in time for dinner. A modicum of freedom sounds great.

But now I'm halfway through my precious solitude. The garden beans are all producing bushels, although they were planted at staggered times. Butter crunch lettuce, red and green peppers, broccoli, beets and cucumbers—almost everything except for the tomatoes is yielding its fruit. My seasonal picking and giving away of the excess begins even without his lists, which include watering, dusting plants, weeding, cultivating and looking for enemies. I'm delighted that the shiny beetles that love to nibble on raspberry and grape leaves are fewer in number this year—especially since the beetle traps Fritz purchased are still in cellophane. The birds have pecked at only a few strawberries—no need for the string of whirling CD disks this year. Deer, bunnies and ground hogs have not broached the newly submerged chicken-wire fence that surrounds the garden. So I'm lulled into thinking we will not be at war this year.

Not so—there's a hidden foe. Before Fritz left, I discovered a zucchini plant that was vibrant one day, then curled and quite dead the next. Then another. We cast them into the proverbial fire. Now zucchini aren't primo on anyone's list, but when the bug or fungus moved over to the acorn squash that were leafing and budding outside the fence, fear heightened. Dusting with an organic powder seemed to do the trick—that is, until Fritz said his goodbyes. Now I'm on the watch for the droop of leaves on stiff stems, which are already sprouting baby squash amid more yellow-orange squash blossoms.

The only cure is pulling up the dying plants by the roots to abort the invaders' spread. I have trouble killing anything, even when it is necessary, just so that other plants can live. Oh no! Is that the first sign of the wilt on the pickles and cucumbers too? I can't bring myself to spoil the fisherman's fun with this news, so when he calls I assure him that everything is just fine. Do I feel guilty about the lie or just because I couldn't do anything to stop the slow death? I want to go on strike—but then who would pull up the dead plants?

Serendipity: Daughter Barb just gave me a gorgeous new cookbook for my birthday. I browsed the dedication page of *Homegrown Pure and Simple* to find the following poetic gush over nature from the writer to his mother:

> "For you (Mom) I have only one question:
> why didn't you tell me about
> those damned squash borers?
> No worries, I'll let you know
> when I figure it out for myself."

NATURE WATCH

A small caterpillar caught my eye while he sauntered down the same path I walk every day—the driveway to the mailbox. This little guy is not new—I noticed him last year too—but he is such a sight. I had to stop and peer again for a while. He is short by "cat" standards, maybe one-and-a-half inches long, and has a segmented, fuzzy body. There are two main segments, each made up of about a dozen parts. The parts are black with yellow marks, like a wide V. Of course he has many legs, one attached to each part for fast and agile movement (it's hard to think walking when describing that many legs and feet moving in sync). But the real mark of distinction is his little antennae, four of them—one protruding from either side of each end.

When I watched him too long, I think he sensed my eyes and felt danger. He rolled himself into a coin-like circle so he would look entirely different—almost inanimate. I'm terribly curious about the creature he will become. Will he be plain in comparison to his fancy features now, or will he become the most colorful and striking butterfly to flit across the prairie as the cool days of fall creep over us? I wish I knew, but in such a wide-open setting his metamorphosis will undoubtedly remain a mystery hidden from my view.

• • •

Another creature drew my attention. When flying, it looked like a winged grasshopper, but I followed its flight between stalks of wild grasses and realized it was entirely different.

It had a long, narrow body and wings that covered it while resting. Its color was protective, matching the stalk so precisely that I would never have seen it but for its flight. It looked like a tiny, tan praying mantis, but I suppose it was a species all its own. I'll be surprised if I ever see this insect again; perhaps this is to be our first and the last encounter. How sad!

• • •

Later—Oops, I was wrong about the beetle traps. From my window I've been seeing yellow—not of prairie coneflowers, black-eyed Susans or primroses, but more like a sign. After Fritz came back from Alaska, he called me to come look at something. It seems that the yellow I had seen was the plastic top of a beetle-bag trap that is now half full of those iridescent, hard-shelled beetles that love grape and raspberry leaves! Not that I can put aside my own container with soap water because I still see some moth-like holes on leaves. So with something like glee, I slip my jar under a copulating pair and flick the branch to dislodge them, forcing the critters down for their last swim. I am an executioner with no remorse.

The Flat Iron Serengeti

"It's like the Serengeti here... I keep waiting for a wild animal to jump out of the bush!" were the words of a smiling Fed-Ex driver. "Is this your first time out here?" I ask, knowing that unless you observe the growth over the summer months,

this final fullness can come as quite a surprise. The driveway bordered by little bluestem and flanked by taller grasses resembles a tunnel or a covered bridge—especially at night, when the headlights accent foliage on either side. And then near the house there is a forest of late summer flowers.

His question made me look at the landscape with fresh eyes. The stiff goldenrod stands as tall as my shoulder, and the prairie coneflower even taller. The rain garden is so full of tall flowers (should I call them weeds?), like ironweed, Joe pye weed and swamp milkweed, that you might imagine the ground level with the drive instead of a sunken garden. Even without much rain these plants flourish, along with the sunflowers near the lower garden path—and then, seemingly out of nowhere, a burst of wild asters. The contrast between the intense, golden-orange clusters and the delicate violet petals is a fitting finale, a last splash of color at the end of August here on the Flat Iron Serengeti.

Clouds: Big with Mercy

When we first moved to this patch of land, I was impressed with the clouds. Seeing them at each different time of year in this "big sky country" (not Montana, but with the same feel) prompted me to write a series of meditations about them with the above title. Although this one reflects clouds at a different time of year, I include it because it captures my initial desire to write about what I see.

Rising with the Sun

"God came…His glory covered the heavens and his praise filled the earth. His splendor was like the sunrise; rays flashed from his hand, where his power was hidden." (Habakkuk 3:3–4)

If I could predict beautiful sunrises, I wouldn't have to keep a morning vigil in my darkened kitchen. Weather people are no help. The things they can predict, like temperature and precipitation, and even the time of sunrise or sunset, don't solve this problem. I want to know in advance whether the conditions are right for color in the sky. If they could alert me to upcoming beauty, as they do with meteor showers, I'd be in my ringside seat.

My husband thinks it a bit strange to see me sitting in the dark kitchen, my chair facing the window. He enjoys waiting less than I, especially when there's a chance the parade will pass us by.

There are a few clues as I walk the dog in the predawn light. Clouds are good signs this morning, a week after the winter solstice. The sun will be late in coming, but the flattened egg of a moon still glows. The air feels crisp, clear. Hope rises while I brew a cup of tea and take up my observation post at the large window facing east. The finches, both scarlet and mustard yellow, amuse me while I look over the lake, through bare trees, and begin to notice a tinge of pink on the underside of clouds. Without fanfare, the color above, where the sun will be, spreads until the clouds ripple richly, while an invisible brush coats others in both directions.

Glorious color everywhere. As pink melds into orange, I know this morning's show is almost over.

In much the same way, if I could predict when my writing muse is likely to appear, I could set a date and be there expectantly. No waiting around. No wasting time. We'd be punctual and productive, my computer and I.

Before I became a writer, I read with horror about persons rising at five in the morning, long before today's eight o'clock sunrise, bundling in sweaters and wool socks, and trudging with coffee in hand upstairs for a morning write. All that before the real work of the day begins. I knew it would take a miracle for me to habitually leave my warm bed hours before I had to. Sunrises and inspiration come at their own time. But if I'm not there, I'll miss them totally. So I go regularly, albeit after dawn, to the desk and wait, now with my back to the window and every sense focused on the blank page. Some days I sit alone. No spark of color or form appears. But I'm still there, expectantly ready for beauty to happen.

"Write down the revelation and make it plain on tablets so that a herald may run with it. For the revelation awaits an appointed time; it speaks of the end and will not prove false. Though it linger, wait for it; it will certainly come and will not delay." (Habakkuk 2:2–3)

Prairie Coneflowers

"From everyone who has been given much, much will be demanded; and from the one who has been entrusted with much, much more will be asked." (Luke 12:48b)

So you think you want to win the lottery… until you do. Having sudden abundance is not easy to handle, as many lottery winners can attest. Abundance of anything forces decision-making: what to do with the excess—build bigger barns? Hide it in the ground? Use it quickly? Give it away? You never know until you have it that abundance can be a burden as well as a blessing. Most successful gardeners soon find that they can't possibly eat all the food they produce. Nor can they simply save the excess until a recipient can be found because it has to be picked and cleaned and stored or it will spoil. Preserving food by canning, freezing or drying is time-consuming. Abundance of zucchini and tomatoes are the greatest challenge; just when you have way too many, so do others.

Here on the prairie we're reminded of abundance, especially in August. The earth has brought forth towering grasses, like big bluestem; the field is full of prairie coneflowers and horsemint. When plants perk up after a "shower of blessing" (see Ezekiel 34:26), we are reminded of water's vital role in plentitude. When the ragweed goes to seed, we remember that the air is filled with many things we can't see, including dangerous pollutants. We don't often think about the soil's health until it washes away with erosion. Water, air and soil are elements that need our care as much as the plants we tend.

And as we've learned from the way invasive plants spread, oodles of flowers, however lovely, are not always a blessing. More food than we can use could bless others if it's well placed. Financial resources, talents, material possessions and even abundant experiences are given in order to be used—the burden and the joy of plentitude. We hold abundance in trust— a burden that only giving can relieve.

Learn more: Frazer Valley Gleaners: www.fvgleaners.org One of several Canadian Christian initiatives to glean and dry excess produce to make portable soup packets for developing countries.

September morn

We danced until the night became a brand new day

Two lovers playing scenes from some romantic play

September morning still can make me feel this way.

Neil Diamond

New England Asters

September Beginnings: Starting up, starting over, beginning again: All hold equal hopefulness. My best time is first thing in the morning, and my best days have always been: the day after a big project was completed, the day after Sunday, the day after December 31. I also love the day after the last day of summer. My late August birthday signals not only the beginning of another year of life for me but also the beginning of a school year, even though the classroom scene has not replayed for me since graduate school some twenty years ago. Back-to-school ads fill the newspaper. The buzz of the grandchildren affects me as they anticipate a new teacher and a new grade and sometimes a new school.

I may not be going back to school, but the school year clock still ticks permanently within me after decades of conditioning. A school year is like a textbook containing the ingredients of a course—a distinct chunk of information of unknown potential. The new academic year is a blank slate waiting to be written upon.

"God came…His glory covered the heavens and his praise filled the earth. His splendor was like the sunrise; rays flashed from his hand, where his power was hidden."

(Habakkuk 3:3–4)

I make more New Year's resolutions in September than I do on New Year's Day. My blackboard is clean, but I have the chalk in my hand, as I did during my brief foray as a grade school teacher. What will I pin on the tag boards? At fall's beginning I can color anything onto their surface. The fresh page is neither clouded nor crowded by all those unfinished projects from last school year; the time for them passed as the August calendar was ripped off, revealing blocks of unblemished newness. In September I'll mark the days that pass, not by an X over a box, but by journaling some detail of life lived in each small square of time. Hope rises when a whole new month of still-empty squares spreads out before me.

On that first cool day of September fall is already in the air, as green bushes and trees slowly begin to take on golds and crimsons. Nature is turning the corner. On the prairie, summer lingers. With favorable moisture, sun and temperature, the wildflowers will continue to bloom and the grasses wave in the wind as they change color on their seeding tips. Their next beginning must wait until spring, but mine can start today.

Seeing Again As Though for the First Time

Six days without walking down the driveway. During four of them I was away providing childcare for some grandchildren, and the last two were spent recovering from the cold I brought back home. That's one part about fall I had conveniently forgotten—all those kids bringing their bugs together at school, spreading them around—and then sharing them with the family. I got some of the leftovers.

I bundle up even on this warm day and slowly walk the walk. Everything is new: a bird calling a new song over the swale; new white flowers resembling the feathery fleabane but with petals that are rounded slightly toward the center; and the grasses sporting new bronze hues. My feet feel the pavement below as though for the first time, and my body happily comes along.

The big bluestem stand tall. They've put on height, as well as multiplied, while I was gone. I'm reminded of that story I've heard about the prairies of the Great Plains before they were disturbed for other uses. A person on horseback could get lost among the big bluestem because the plants were taller than the both of them. When we first came to this land the cornstalks were that tall, but at least they were in rows

The Perfect Pod

that could be followed to find a way out. But imagine being surrounded by glasses taller than yourself on the flat Great Plains and not being able to spot a landmark. It would be more like being at sea than on land. Maybe that was the real reason for those long, feathered Indian tomahawks.

The little bluestem has also changed. Silvery seeds now cover each stalk of each cluster. The stems blow wildly, but the seeds seem to hang on until they're manually harvested. Behind them are the milkweed and butterfly weed pods popping open to let out their seeds, each holding an inverted umbrella and ready to ride the wind. Just before they fly, one can see the intricate layering of the seeds within the pod— a beauty to behold. The milkweed leaves have turned from green to yellow and soon will turn as brown as their hanging pods. Sometimes Fritz thinks we should discourage the growth of so much milkweed—until he is reminded that the butterflies would go somewhere else if our milkweed way-station were not here. With that many little propeller seeds blowing around, I can't imagine making a dent in their propagation.

Goldenrod dot the field haphazardly, and a few purple asters have found their way along the path. Near the main road, I notice that the sumac trees have sprouted their thick maroon clusters of seeds, resembling little, painted Christmas trees. Soon, as fall advances, their leaves will also turn maroon.

Peering around from within my usual nature trance, I notice a woman walking toward me at an exercise pace.

Thinking it's my neighbor, Pam, I stop so she won't think I'm rude for only waving. The woman is not Pam, but now I must say something. She stops, and we introduce and quickly begin talking, as though we've known each other for a while. She is doing the same round-the-block that I do, only beginning from a different point. It's fun finding out that we have many connections.

I tell her how surprised I've been over the years that rural neighbors tend to stay to themselves as much as those in the city. She agrees but shares that she and her husband have found a bit of a community among a cluster of three houses off their drive. Soon I know many things about her family and she about mine. Her teenage son, who is a senior, has mono and pneumonia, which have wiped out his cherished hopes of playing football. She was a single mother at sixteen but has gone on to marry, put her husband through college, and have two more children. We have roots in the same religious traditions. Before I know it, we've talked for half an hour. I have to get busy with supper. "See you later," I announce wishfully—almost, I think, as a question—as she walks on, both of us probably wondering Will I ever see her again? Did we plant enough seeds for friendship? I see the possibilities even in this rural place.

NATURE WATCH | *Treasures*

In the garden yesterday, while I stooped to find zucchini among the abundant foliage, something that looked like a broken stalk—moved. I may have surprised it, but it certainly surprised me as well as it slithered away. I had never before encountered a snake in the garden. This one looked big, but when I pulled back the plants I couldn't find him. Soon after this chance encounter, I heard a soft rattling sound. "Are there rattlesnakes in Michigan? Do other, less dangerous snakes make sounds like a rattle too?" I asked Fritz. He didn't know, but once you imagine a possibility it's hard not to start hearing gourd-like rattles and soft slithers under every bush.

X Marks the Spot

"The kingdom of heaven is like treasure hidden in the field. When a man found it, he hid it again, and then in his joy went and sold all he had and bought that field." (Matthew 13:44)

Even before we moved onto the land near Flat Iron Lake, we had heard the story of Chief Wabasis. A nearby north/south road is named after this Indian chief who, as legend would have it, once buried treasure somewhere near the lake. No one seems to know where the treasure was hidden or whether it would be considered valuable by today's standards, but just the word treasure has been intriguing enough to compel kids of all ages to search. My imagination pictures a metal box with a bell-shaped, curved top, like one a pirate might have found on a treasure island.

When the grandkids get restless, we resurrect the legend and send them off with shovels. The most metal they've discovered has been on a little slope at the mouth of the woods that was once used as a dump for household refuse. The quest for metal (think money or jewels) soon gives way to a search for wild berries and animal tracks, not to mention those thick vines that are so much fun to swing on.

Spontaneous Combustion on the Prairie

I work on the second floor of our house next to high windows, the view from which I try to ignore while I write. During a particularly dramatic thunderstorm I raced down to the lower level and suggested to Fritz that he turn off his computer just to be safe, after which I hurried back up to do the same with mine. Glancing out my window at the black sky and the expanse of prairie being drenched below, I suddenly spied smoke rising from the center of the section behind the swale. Not only is it rare to see smoke anytime other than when we purposefully burn the prairie, but it's unheard of in the midst of a downpour. But there it was, billowing upward from somewhere near the mowed path. I called Fritz, panic in my voice, and he came running. Extremely dry weather before this rain had made for abundant fuel on the ground.

Fritz grabbed a broom-rake, jumped on his golf cart, and headed in the direction of the smoke. I was instructed to get the phone and be ready to call the fire department if he couldn't extinguish the flames. There were indeed little, licking flames beneath the smoke, despite the heavy rain. Fritz thrashed at them, and they gave up quickly enough from the combination of the beating and the water. Fritz, who hadn't taken the time to put on his shoes, came back drenched from bare head to bare toe. No one knows how the fire started, but we speculate that lightning grounded there. We're somewhat surprised, as this was a low spot with no metal present. Perhaps there are mineral deposits under the surface. Or hey, maybe we've found the site of Chief Wabasis' buried treasure! Is it too late to mark the spot?

Sharing the Loot

A powerful storm passed though last night, the kind that can fell even healthy trees. We looked for damage on our acreage. Near the road there's a nice stand of trees on one side of a gully that often has water running through it in the springtime. A grove of hickory is nestled among the other trees, producing an abundance of small, soft-shelled nuts. We saw that one part of a magnificent timber had either been torn down by wind or hit by lightning. It looked as though a giant hand had torn it from the tree but then left it before it was all the way detached. We observed a moment of silence beside the mortally wounded tree. It's hard to lose even one of our sheep.

After the world dried out, we returned to gather hickory nuts. We picked a half-bushel, knowing that many more remained for squirrel food. We put ours on the far side of our garage, planning to harvest the nutmeats later on. We had never had squirrels near the house so figured they were safe; just in case, though, we kept the doors closed. Still, the level seemed to go down. One day a nearly empty bushel caught Fritz's eye, and he silently scolded both the squirrels and himself for our own procrastination.

But that was not the end of the nuts. Winter came along, and with it the need to turn on the heat in our cars. Fritz complained that the ventilation system wasn't working properly in his car, and he could see a fine powder on the dashboard. But before he brought it in to the dealer, I thought I noticed the same residue in the other car. The service shop declared the system to be working fine, but the dust kept coming. Finally, the mechanic took apart the whole system, after which he showed me something neither he nor anyone else in the shop had ever before seen: a tray full of half-gnawed hickory nuts and mouse droppings!

The warm underside of the car must have seemed the perfect location to throw a nutty mouse party. So much for "nutting."

Who Rules My Life?

"For where your treasure is, there your heart will be also," Jesus declared. (Matthew 6:21) Isn't it amazing that the first thing that came to my mind when the lightning struck and started a fire was buried treasure? What, I wonder, does that say about my values? Walking this land daily and assimilating all of the beauty and natural gifts should lift me to a higher plain. And the experience does for a while, until I come back to my desk and try to record what I see and feel. That's when temptation hits: The machine I work on can do other things too. It brings me messages from around the world—today there was one from Nairobi, Kenya.

I now use a portable Mac computer that has a dock on the lower edge of the screen with symbols, useful for getting me from one place to another with a single click. Safari™ (Mac's Internet designation) means "journey," and I find that I can effortlessly travel to any newspaper, news report, or live video I choose. Words and pictures my parents used to search for the hard way are at my fingertips. When was the last time I looked up any piece of information in the hardcover Encyclopedia Britannica?

The other night, my husband wondered why I was always looking at my computer while watching TV. "It's just like reading the newspaper," I replied, "only it comes electronically." Even when I don't prefer to watch his show, I like to be in the same place, and this seemed like a good alternative. My magazines are stacked there for the same

purpose. Maybe they'll all be online one day, and I'll never have to recycle another bundle.

But something greater is at work. Because the computer is set for Google news, I instantly get the rundown and can jump from there to any number of other stories, based on their titles. Soon I'm "surfing the net" a practice I used to disparage. I can see now how easy it is to become addicted to anything that interests me—it's all so accessible. For me it's still mostly about reading, but pictures offer a convenient shortcut, and YouTube™ produces short videos at a click.

So, while I'm supposed to be concentrating on the work at hand, I can't wait more than a few seconds to pull up a new piece of mail (that tiny number on the icon entices me). Then there's the promise of news, just waiting for my attention at any time. During this election year, things change so rapidly, and I want to know at all times what's going on.

But wait! I can remember back to a time when I refused a pager at work because it would interrupt my concentration. If people really want to find me, I had reasoned, let them leave me a message, and I'll get back to them. Now I carry a cell phone whenever I leave home. There was a time when you had to be home to watch a TV show at a certain time—now there's the recorder. Remember when that little transistor radio with its notoriously poor reception was the only portable listening device? Now there are smaller and smaller pods hanging around everyone's neck. And the camera—does anyone remember what film looks like? What would the TV stations do without pictures being transmitted instantaneously from various hot spots with phone cameras? Pretty soon we won't even have to charge our devices; this will be done wirelessly.

I'll admit that it's not just the kids who need to get unplugged and unglued from one screen or another. I don't want to be left behind, either, unable to use or understand the new media. But some of my age-mates have for the most part given up on the newest toys. The answering machine is high-tech enough.

Where is my treasure? Knowledge, access and convenience give me a rush. Now that I know how they feel, I wonder whether I could survive without them. Election Day is coming—I think I'll set November 4 as the beginning of my Lenten-type withdrawal from electronic devices. Up-to-the-minute news won't seem as vital then. Well, on second thought, if I can't give them up altogether, at least I'll try to make a rational decision of how and when to disconnect before it's too late.

"God has been wireless from the beginning. We can always be in touch."

Thank goodness for that walk down the driveway every day. What a rush; what a treasure—and of a totally different, and even opposite kind! The landscape changes with the seasons, but the Creator never does. I don't even have to carry a battery pack—God has been wireless from the beginning. We can always be in touch.

JOURNAL ENTRY

9/22/08—Instead of beginning the day at the desk, I started in the garden, picking raspberries and beans for my brother-in-law, so Fritz could stop with a gift after a meeting in town. I know the produce will brighten Ted's day a little. Today marks four months since Ted's kidney transplant, but the new organ is only sputtering along. Three years ago Fritz had the same procedure but with a live donor, and he improved immediately and is now healthy, despite requiring high levels of anti-rejection drugs. As I pull the red berries off the white cones that hold them, I'm overwhelmed by thoughts of disease and death. One friend has ALS; his wife and kids do everything they can for his comfort, but he is steadily declining. A writer friend sent an e-mail telling me of finishing her book while coping with painful fibromyalgia, praying all the while that it isn't actually multiple sclerosis.

Late Raspberries

Discovering Purpose

For the last twenty-seven years, after surviving a sudden, nearly fatal bout of internal bleeding, I've been free from pain and disease. But with sickness all around, touching my heart if not my own body, I'm sober about life. I look around at the groundcover, the wild grasses and the trees all changing color in one last splash of brilliance—before they begin to slowly die. I wonder whether they are resigned to their fate. Or perhaps making a statement: "Even the end can be glorious!"

I try to hang on to life in the growing things all around me, all the while aware that their life is also fleeting. I think about those lines in Psalm 103:16 about the flower of the field: "The wind blows over it and it is gone, and its place remembers it no more." Frost warnings are coming soon; low temperatures will end the growing season. Perennial plants will re-seed themselves and pop up again next year, whether or not I'm here to cheer them on. But the annuals need a gardener. Fritz talks about making the garden more manageable next year, but I take a wait-and-see attitude. Some days when picking and preserving wear me down, I wonder whether I'm up to another demanding year of harvesting. The glow seems somehow to be slipping off the pumpkin.

The real issue: How will I spend the time left for me—the days and seasons before the wind passes over me and I, too, am gone? Not to ponder that question is to deny

Indian Grass Going to Seed

that death, maybe preceded by disease, will come to me. My plans for fall now incorporate a sense of urgency. What is important? Why? Am I chasing after the wind so it won't turn around and overtake me?

Yesterday's sermon was about Jesus "meeting" Lazarus—four days after Lazarus's death. The family and friends of the dead Lazarus met Jesus not with joy but with what sounded like scolding but may have been wistful, and wishful, thinking: "If only you had been here…" They wanted him to take away death. Jesus wanted to tell them something about himself: He too would die.

Jesus lived and died for a purpose. Do I? Will I? I want to think so—but after seventy years I still find it hard to tell anyone precisely what that purpose is. Perhaps these later-in-life thoughts are common, and they may be the very reason my dad struggled as he approached old age. He too questioned both his accomplishments and his purpose on this Earth.

Searching for the last berries and the last ingathering of beans, my reflection sometimes gives rise to thoughts that I have missed the mark, that I have not been or done what God had hoped for me. But then when I straighten up and look over the vast fields, I recognize that I'm only a small part of God's grand scheme of life. This despite the fact that I often feel like the center of something—if not the universe, then of some tiny sphere of influence and association: teaching, sharing, writing—and, in some small way—loving.

The flower of the field withers but one seed lasts forever: "…you must love one another intensely and with a pure heart. For you have been born again, not by a seed that perishes but by one that cannot perish—by the living and everlasting word of God." (1 Peter 1:22–23 ISV)

For, "All human life is like grass,
and all its glory is like a flower in the grass.
The grass dries up and the flower drops off,
but the word of the Lord lasts forever."
Now this word is the good news that was
announced to you. (1 Peter 1:24–25 ISV)

In the end I hear the announcement: I am only one soul seeking to be faithful. And I know that God's love for me and others is unrelated to any of our accomplishments. He simply enjoys what is pleasing within his creation and lavishes grace. I will never stop wondering about the meaning and purpose of my life but will enjoy the good news of my rebirth in Christ from the beginning, through the middle, and to the glorious end, here at Flat Iron Lake.

Black Swallowtail Butterfly

Beauty and the Beast

Consider what a great forest is set on fire by a small spark. (James 3:5b)

It's still dark as I drag the last plastic bag into the garage and slam the door of the rental car. Driving south from my aged mother's home in Ft. Collins to Denver International Airport to catch an early flight, I watch the sunrise develop in the east. The light and color slowly intensify in the September sky, catching the undersides of layers of clouds. If the highway were not a straight arrow, driving for me would be dangerous—so deep in thought but enamored as I am with the orange-gold-red glow. I force myself to devote equal attention to brake lights ahead as the traffic thickens toward Denver. "Is every morning a light-show like this?" I wonder.

At the height of color, just before the sun clears the horizon, its rays find a break in the clouds and shoot straight upward—a sun pillar—to usher in the finale. With the same suddenness, a sharp odor fills my throat and nose. My eyes begin to water. As the eastern clouds take me in, I approach dark, ominous clouds on the west. It takes a minute to recognize it: not a storm cloud but a fire cloud. The forest fires near Boulder had finally been contained the night before, sending their soot-laden clouds away from the mountains.

Beauty and the beast on either side of the road, divided by a thread. Inspiration and ugliness. It's much too simplistic to conclude that God's natural wonders are beautiful but that humanity's careless use of them chars the Earth and ruins creation. Most forest fires are sparked by lightning, which humans can neither make nor control, and then are fed by wind racing through over-dry forests.

Like the smoke, I'm heading away from the Rockies, where I have helped Mom sort through papers and pictures and tiny mementos before her move from a condo to a single room in a retirement center. At times, I think a sudden fire would be more merciful than the deliberate depositing, piece by piece, of her treasures into a trash bag. The past is not easily laid aside.

The sky's contrasts catch me off guard. How can God hold unlike things together: making Technicolor skies through breaks in the clouds, while carrying away fire debris on black, noxious clouds at the same time and place? Both demand my attention: triumph and tragedy, colorful life and grimy death, memories past and an unknown future—separated by a double line on I-25.

As morning breaks, I pray for grace to see God clearly on both sides of the highway.

Environmental Notes | *Ecology's Mandate*

Children in a special environmental school were each assigned one square foot of ground to care for and learn from for a year. Week after week the fifth graders visited their land to observe what was happening over seasons, in myriad weather/light conditions, and at different times of the day. They watched, listened, touched, smelled and sometimes tasted the earth in all its fullness, much as Annie Dillard has done at Tinker Creek. They studied not only the surface but also the underside of the turned soil. Their senses were heightened by unhurried concentration on one small slice of the Earth. They became hunters and gatherers of ecological knowledge within the wordless, articulate book of creation.

As one environmentalist has noted, we can put one foot down on a piece of ground and have no idea of all of the life that coexists there with our own. One lesson the kids learned is that all of life is interconnected, that even a slight alteration of one element affects all others. Each living thing is important for the well-being of other organisms, and its environment is an active life force. Air, light, water and even fire play their part in furthering the natural life cycle.

It's hard to be a passive observer of nature, once you've experienced it at eye level. As awareness heightens, so does concern. Are the things we do helping or hurting the environment? Has expansion of roads, homes, towns and technology enhanced the connectedness of the species or broken important links? And how fragile is the tie between humans and the natural world they inhabit?

An ecosystem is dependent upon the movement of energy and matter through itself. One increasingly popular way to trace the connection between systems or species has to do with their roles in the food chain. Who eats what (or whom) tells us a lot about interconnectedness. Barbara Kingsolver has raised our awareness of "buying local." Added to the cost of food (and sometimes subtracting from the food value) are transportation, fuel and packaging. Co-op farms are springing up, offering fresh food in season, in conjunction with an obligation to play a part in its growth and harvesting. More of us are becoming producers as well as consumers.

A recent issue of *Science* featured Restorative Ecology, the idea of returning nature to its original state. Documented "ages" of the Earth show that in order to be truly "original," one would have to return to creation—an obvious impossibility. The best-case scenario might be a restoration of a balance in which life flourishes, along with an effort aimed at reducing the fallout from civilization's progress.

Learn more:
Animal, Vegetable, Miracle by Barbara Kingsolver
Ecology facts for kids—www.idahoreports.org/dialogue4kids

October

Sunrise, sunset

Sunrise, sunset

Swiftly fly the years

One season following another

Laden with happiness and tears.

Fiddler on the Roof

Sunrise over Flat Iron Lake

ALL NATURE SINGS: A SPIRITUAL JOURNEY OF PLACE

October Reflections: I've come full circle, a year of pilgrimage: I've walked through twelve months, 365 days and countless hours and minutes. No two days have been the same; each was filled with unexpected veers and wiggles, even though my path never changed. This has been a year of being filled with curiosity, wonder, expectation and a measure of dread. I didn't "seek new landscapes," as Proust once observed, but instead followed his advice and opened new eyes. The act of recording my thoughts, in season and within one year, helped me see my pilgrimage as a journey both in time and in place. Reclaiming earlier writing and sprinkling it into its seasonal place, despite the varying vantage points in terms of years, added a dimension of more years than just this one. Reliving the journey of our ten years here, I'm reminded of how the richness of my life on this land has grown over time.

I still live with the dreamer. Dreams rarely come true, but this one has. The prairie has taken on a personality all its own, and now that it's established I often see him observing it from a distance, as one would watch his grown children. Beauty startles the planter; taking credit for any of it would be presumptuous. This place is a gift, just like grace. We could never have imagined such serenity in the midst of the often-unsettling news of the day. That wonderful Hebrew word Shalom describes it well, especially in October when the work is done and the farmer/restorer retreats to his desk.

The real voyage of discovery consists not in seeking new landscapes, but in having new eyes.

Marcel Proust

Maybe during the dark months he'll reread his old favorite by Willa Cather, *O Pioneers!* Or *Silent Spring* by Rachel Carson, a book that once goaded him to do his part to take care of this earth. This might be the winter he'll respond to my prodding and write his own tribute to the land around Flat Iron Lake. But soon enough the seed catalogs will start coming, and he'll begin dreaming about next year's garden. He'll consider the fields and pick the plots for spring burning. He'll select his best bird and bloom pictures and enhance them on the computer.

One day we may ask each other, while watching the evening news, "How many more years can this place be our home?" We'll resist predictions in the hope that many good years still lie ahead for us. We've planned for the day when the house and the land will be too much for us, but the harder part will be to ease that thought into our hearts. Leaving a place you love is like finishing a book; you're reluctant to write that last word or to read the last chapter before putting it away on the shelf.

SIGHTINGS | *Hart on Hart St.*

Long before we bought this field, the owner picked a spot for the drive off the main road to gain access to the property. A little stream, boisterous in early spring, complicated the selection on either side of what has become our driveway entrance. At one point a culvert was placed under the main road, right at the lowest point that flooded regularly. The culvert solved the problem for humans, but evidently not for deer. This point is also their natural trail through the woods, which is now separated by the pavement of Hart Street.

Not long after we moved here Hart was resurfaced, and the road commission put up a new guardrail opposite our drive where the terrain drops off precipitously. Again, the rail was good for humans, who might otherwise stray onto the narrow shoulder, but not good for deer, who follow their thirst for the first running water of the season along familiar paths. The result: carnage of deer on the very street that bears their "older" name. I've lost count of the deer/car confrontations near our driveway.

One Sunday morning before I had walked to get the paper, a man knocked on the door asking, "Got yourself a deer?" He must have come by the drive soon after a car killed a deer and wanted permission to carry it away—for food. We went to examine the crime scene—blood everywhere, and pieces of car body and a side mirror strewn along this infamous corridor. Since some of them were jagged glass and metal, we had to pick up each one or risk a punctured tire.

One accident involved two deer hit by one car, but the most spectacular was the deer/motorcycle accident. A man on a speeding bike hit a deer, sending both himself and the vehicle careening up the side hill from the impact. Somehow the driver walked away, but for many weeks the plastic front shield of his bike lay up the bank as a haunting reminder.

The other day as I turned onto Hart for my morning walk around the block, three hart stood on the pavement about a hundred yards away. I stopped, and we stared at each other for a few moments. A quiet step or two on my part, and their ears perked, listening to the sounds I had made. I've heard that they don't see well but that smell is their most dominant sense. So I can probably blame my pre-shower scent for their sudden leap over another guardrail and their crashing flight through the trees and brush below. People can watch for cars and step aside for oncoming danger in the form of traffic. I wish deer-harts could sense the danger of machines and run before the inevitable collision on Hart Street. If the reality of this danger could be imprinted upon them and passed along to succeeding generations, as our electric fence has been (see "November") fewer car/deer accidents would leave the doe dead beside the road, unable to warn her young, as my mother always did: "Look both ways before you cross the street."

Hart Street has no deer crossing sign, but the potential for an encounter is imprinted on some of our minds. Especially on the minds of those who have already lost a car or repair money because they hit a deer on some country road like Hart. I hope others notice the name of this road as they turn onto it; otherwise, I fear they'll learn its origin soon enough, in an unforgettable way.

Nature's Outhouse

As the grasses grow even taller, the asphalt driveway has become nature's outhouse. Scat of peculiar sizes and shapes, scattered here and there, is hard to ignore. So I become a detective: What kind of an animal could have left this pile? With a morbid fascination, like a clue hunter on *CSI,* I imagine the critters that decide to dump on the drive. Footprints in snow are mysterious too, but they are easier to identify than these blackened stool samples. The pebbled refuse of plant-eaters like deer and rabbit is the easiest to decipher. But, could this one be from one of the night prowlers—raccoon or possum—or one of the day stalkers, like fox or coyote?

Yesterday a cat scurried across my path. Oh, yes—the drive is also nature's litter box. How convenient—no mess or cleanup for tabby's owner. But I don't run for a pooper-scooper because nature provides its own recycling program—even of scat. I can't help but watch one pile that has attracted dozens of black and red bugs that will carry away the dung, morsel by tiny morsel.

I do sympathize with the animals that must try to find a spot to squat among the thick wild grasses. Jake has a similar problem in winter, when his leap into the "bushes" leaves him up to his belly in snow. So it shouldn't be too surprising that year around, as the blacktop absorbs heat during the day, it offers nothing short of a heated outhouse for our animal friends living among us. Be our guests. I'll watch my step.

Sounds I Can't Ignore

My open office window lets in prairie sounds and smells on this mid-October day. Indian Summer has thrilled us for three days with temps nearing eighty degrees. An occasional chirp or bee buzz does not distract me, but a frenzied "caw, caw," followed by an equally wild response from another bird drew me to the window. I was just in time to see four or five blackbirds going after a much larger hawk. Perhaps they were fighting over some delicious carcass. The hawk, clearly outnumbered, took refuge in the tall cottonwood by the swale, and the blackbirds retreated to the waterfront willows. I don't know who won the prize or returned to the kill, or whether any of the combatants were wounded. All I know is that their startling noise on a blissful day set me to wondering.

A Circle of Trees
October, 2002

Fall is here. I can no longer watch the leaves change from a distance. It's time to enter the forest. As I step inside the canopy of trees, I think back to April's foray into the woods when the younger grandchildren and I explored the thick underbrush, looking for signs of spring.

Their excitement filled the cool air. Who will discover the first jack-in-the-pulpit, or trillium or spring beauty? I tell them about watching for the blossom on the May apple, under whose broad leaves I always wished to find morel mushrooms on wet mornings. Morgan notices the ferns unrolling like feathery yoyos. The winter has left twigs, limbs and even logs across our path. Little Dani nearly stumbles over a log of dirt raised by the burrowing moles. We look up through the tall trees of this mature forest, not yet fully leafed, and see blue. Soon the light will have to weave through thick growth to warm the forest earth. We can already hear the toads peeping from the bog. Through the eyes of children all nature looks new.

That April day I was glad the little girls and I didn't have to walk all the way. Distances are great on our acreage, so I didn't fuss when my husband brought home a battered but functional golf cart. I prefer to walk, but the little machine is a great workhorse, ready to haul tools to the lake or field or just between the barn and the house. There's no point in being a purist when there's work to do, and on fifty acres there's

always plenty. The plodding cart moves at just the right speed for taking my aged mother into the woods so that she, despite her fading eyesight, can move among the tall trees and let them sprinkle their colorful leaves on her back. And I'll admit that, when my troubled feet can't navigate the uneven terrain, the cart still gives me access to the sanctuary of trees. In early spring a load of small grandkids can be dumped at the opening to the woods, ready to explore.

Only thirteen-year-old Lindsay is allowed to drive the cart alone. Today, in October, as I enter the forest unaccompanied, I remember that on one of the last days of summer Lindsay and Matt asked whether they could take the cart into the woods. Approval granted, they gathered up some tools and boards and a marking pen, with an air of adventure. They brushed off my questions by saying they were making something for their cousins to find next Sunday when everyone would gather for the gala August-September birthday party. I asked no more questions.

Birthday Sunday dinner, doubling as a party, arrived on a humid, midsummer-like day, with barely a hint of fall. I waited for Lindsay to announce an expedition to the woods, but she did not. Instead, she confided, "Matt and I thought we'd let them discover it for themselves—someday." I begged, but she wouldn't tell.

Not until today do I discover "it" myself on my walk into the woods, in gorgeous October warmth and wind. I am celebrating as I walk carefully over uneven ground next to the woods for the first time since trouble with my foot and then a knee made walking the field impossible. I chafed during months of favoring my usually sturdy legs. The woods call me today in the same mysterious way that mountains and alpine streams did when I was young. Each deliberate step takes me closer to the tall trees and then onto the loop path that my husband keeps mowed with the brush-hog. Glorious color, flickering light and crackle underfoot.

One footpath leads off the main course farther into the woods. So full of my freedom to walk again, I follow the narrow clearing. At the end, as I reluctantly turn to retrace my steps, I see a neatly lettered sign tacked to a large oak: Circle of Trees.

An aura comes over me as I look up and watch the colorful leaves spinning down. I turn in place at the center of this perfectly empty spot, enclosed naturally by oaks, poplars and maple. I imagine a campfire in the center, with storytellers spinning yarns to bright-eyed children.

Suddenly all the magic of reading and telling stories to the grandkids, and their parents before them, comes alive in this place. Characters of the past join me in this circle, neatly bounded by ancient trees. I see royalty and winged creatures, sense danger and rescue, and even hear the kiss of the prince waking a sleeping beauty. The Circle's enchantment rivals that of Narnia or Terabithia.

To be allowed entry into a secret garden is a gift only children can give. I make them a silent promise: I'll handle their imagination with care and respect. I vow to return often to their mysterious shelter, to relive childlike fantasies amid the Circle of Trees.

The End

Mysterious, illusive, unknown
Til it comes
Withered coneflowers of the field,
Doe petrified in headlights,
A planet run its course.

Mom longed to see it
Sought comfort in knowing—
then, without foresight
We held hands to the end.

Like beginnings—no time before time
No glimpse beyond the great divide,
No knowledge before seeing face to face.

Year's end ushers year's beginning.
Hardly time to say good-bye

As I must one day
To this land, these sticks of trees, this frozen earth.

Goodbye—before my last breath
To my wild dreamer—
To the flowers of friendship
Our children, finches and swans,
Bluestem and lupine.

Spring rains—bless blooms for new eyes
Waving grass—stir other hearts
Mere words recount this pilgrimage
Long after my quest is won.

C. Rottman
November, 2008

Making a machine or creating a star or restoring a prairie is only the first step. A machine will end up in the dump if its moving parts are not oiled or its worn parts replaced. Stars and planets must be kept in constant motion while held in space by someone in control of the universe. A prairie surrounded by so many foreign species must be protected or there will again be weeds on this land that once the steel plow laid open. Fields full of colorful wildflowers and waving tall grasses are constant reminders of the connection between the Creator and the Sustainer.

Every state has a Department of Natural Resources that monitors what resources we have and how we use them. Resources are precious gifts. Each of us has a part in preservation—of soil and water and air—so that the elements of nature that continue to sustain life don't become endangered assets.

The efforts that restored the land now called Flat Iron Lake Preserve will be lost if it is not maintained. Without periodic burns and vigilance against invasive species, the land will slowly revert to its former state. The job of sustaining this land will be assumed by Calvin College, whose faculty and students have been invaluable resources toward understanding the ecology, as well as the care that is needed for preservation. None of us really possess pieces of this Earth; we're only caretakers—for a while.

Sometimes we debate about which force, nature or nurture, is the stronger determinant of a child's future. The deliberation often ends in a draw, although one or the other perspective rises in prominence based on new evidence. A similar discussion rages around the future of our planet. Is nature so determinative that nothing we do makes a difference for good or ill? Hardly. A delicate balance exists between creating and sustaining. One can argue about the percentage of influence, but both clearly exert a force.

The Creator shows his faithfulness by upholding his creation. We creatures are also called to faithfulness. All the ways in which we have harmed creation, often unwittingly, require our sustained attention to alleviate. We have been entrusted with this world and we are called to be worthy stewards.

The care of the Earth is our most ancient and most worthy, and after all our most pleasing responsibility. To cherish what remains of it and to foster its renewal is our only hope.

Wendell Berry

ACKNOWLEDGMENTS

In 2000, we began this prairie restoration project with a sense of purpose that hid our underlying naivety. We learned slowly, through trial and error, what it takes to encourage native growth on a piece of land. All of our research and planning could not have revealed the trials as well as the joys that the actual experience brought. Ten years later we want to thank two professors in particular, Dave Warners and Randy Van Dragt, from Calvin College for sharing their love of the land and expertise concerning wildflowers and grasses, as well as aquatic, forest and prairie ecology. They turned Flat Iron Lake into an outdoor classroom, exposing many students to the wonders of its natural environment.

Calvin students participated with their teachers in the annual spring burn, invasive plant hunts and impromptu lectures while walking the fields or mucking in the lake. While we struggled to know the common names for wildflowers, they learned the scientific names and all about their amazing variety and propagation. Five students also contributed to our education and their own while living here and conducting Summer Research studies: Matt Dykstra, Travis Ellens, Brent Geurink, Jane Louwsma and Jessica Miller. We hope many more will study the ecology of this place. One Calvin graduate did extensive research on the pre- and post-burn soil of the prairie for her thesis at Western Michigan University. To date, sixty-eight species of wildflowers have been cataloged.

Special thanks to Sally Vander Ploeg of Calvin's Development office who fell in love with the prairie on her frequent visits while working to facilitate efforts to preserve the land in perpetuity. Her work has been invaluable. We applaud President Gaylen Byker of Calvin College for his broad vision for the college, which reaches far beyond bricks and mortar. In order to protect the integrity of the land we eagerly entrust it to those who share our desire to restore and preserve natural places.

We will always be grateful to those who worked to preserve the descriptions and images of Flat Iron Lake Preserve within All Nature Sings: Dirk Wierenga, acquisitions editor; Michelle Krievins-Newman, designer; and Ginny McFadden, copy editor.

Carol and Fritz Rottman